2014
THE BEST MEN'S
STAGE MONOLOGUES

2014
THE BEST MEN'S STAGE MONOLOGUES

Edited by
Lawrence Harbison

SMITH AND KRAUS PUBLISHERS 2014

ISBN: 1-57525-887-0
ISBN: 978-1-57525-887-4
ISSN: 2329-2695

Typesetting and layout by Elizabeth Monteleone
Cover Design: Borderlands Press

A Smith and Kraus book
177 Lyme Road, Hanover, NH 03755
Editorial 603.643.6431 To Order 1.877.668.8680
www.smithandkraus.com

Printed in the United States of America

Table of Contents

Here you will find a rich and varied selection of monologues for men from plays which were produced and/or published in the 2013-2014 theatrical season. Most are for younger performers (teens through thirties) but there are also some excellent pieces for older actors as well. Some are comic (laughs), some are dramatic (generally, no laughs). Some are short, some are long. All represent the best in contemporary playwriting.

Several of the monologues are by playwrights whose work may be familiar to you, such as Terrence McNally, Don Nigro, Jane Martin, Bruce Graham, Sharr White, Rajiv Joseph, Charles Fuller, Mark St. Germain and Emily Mann; others are by exciting up-and-comers such as Joshua Harmon, Mando Alvarado, Jonathan Caren, Ron MacLachlan, Chad Beguelin, Daniel Pearle, Lucas Hnath, Reina Hardy, Dominique Morisseau, Steven Levinson and Crystal Skillman.

Many of the plays from which these monologues have been culled have been published and, hence, are readily available either from the publisher/licensor or from a theatrical book store such as the Drama Book Shop in New York. A few plays may not be published for a while, in which case contact the author or agent to request a copy of the entire text of the play which contains the monologue which suits your fancy. Information on publishers/rights holders may be found in the Rights & Permissions section in the back of this anthology.

Break a leg in that audition! Knock 'em dead in class!

Lawrence Harbison
Brooklyn, NY

A COMMON MARTYR
Michael Weems

Dramatic
Sydney: twenty to twenty-five

Sidney is on a camping trip with friends. He's hunted down by his girlfriend, Kim, and unleashes upon her a pent up diatribe that's been years in waiting.

SIDNEY: Talk . . . .or lecture? Nag. Pester. "Stop looking at birds and start looking at me, Sid." "Not until I see a ring, Sid." "You can't get a job there, I'm staying near my folks, Sid." When do I get to talk? Hmm? I know exactly what you had in mind. Four years in college together. We lived in adjoining dorms. I checked in on you every night before bed and got that oh-so-incredible peck on the lips to carry me through to my next bland day. Talked about getting engaged in our junior year—a nice sized rock that's just like the ones you see in magazines, though nothing that's financially attainable by someone—I don't know—like me. And today we graduated together. The next step is getting married next summer in a lavish gala that your family can't afford. You won't be quite ready for sex, as it truly should be foremost about procreation over enjoyment and you want it to be special. As opposed to following my real passion, I'll go off to law school or some graduate program of which I'll have no interest in whatsoever. After I've gotten my worthless Masters degree, I'll land in some boring ass job where I debate on a daily basis whether to push pencils for another day against jumping head first from the twentieth floor and seeing which one hurts more in the long run. By age thirty and either through my having begged for fifteen years or the grace of God, we'll have sex for the first and last time and you'll pump out a child, never working another day of your life. And if we have a boy, odds are you'll start the whole cycle of breaking him down systematically from day one until he's a flaccid pulp-like cardboard cut-out that his father embodies! No thanks. Not for me.

A Delicate Ship
Anna Ziegler

Dramatic
Nate: late twenties to early thirties

Nate is speaking to his best friend Sarah, on whom he's harbored a crush since childhood, and whose romantic evening with her boyfriend he's interrupted. An increasingly unsettled Nate has insisted that the three of them play a game in which each person guesses the identity taped to his/her forehead. This monologue comes at the culmination of that game, when Nate reveals to Sarah that the identity she's been trying to guess is her own. This represents the first turning point in the play: now it's clear that Nate is in Sarah's apartment on more than just friendly terms and has a true agenda—and is perhaps not in the most emotionally stable frame of mind either.

NATE: Your biggest fear is of losing yourself. Losing yourself to the wrong choices, the wrong men, the wrong jobs, the wrong activity on a summer evening when whatever you're not doing is surely more fun. You know you let your brain lead your heart and you worry this won't make you happy in the end, but losing people you actually love is even worse , right? Losing your dad, which you felt you should have been able to control, losing me, which you're sure will eventually happen if you . . . and we're so important to each other; please know that I know that, and I would never disappear. Not if you let yourself— not if we were . . . You would never let me down. You couldn't. We'd get through it all together; we'd traverse the endless series of days like explorers in a ship made of time itself, its delicate sails moving easily through the churning water . . . And your greatest desire? Easy. To be loved, of course. By everyone. Indiscriminately. Unconditionally. But what you don't know is that my love alone would actually be enough. It always has been; it gets you through much more than you give it credit for. If it weren't for me, for instance, this guy wouldn't be here. We both know that.

(Beat)

It's you, Sarah. You're you. Do you get it?

Information on this playwright may be found at www.smithandkraus.com. Click on the AUTHORS tab.

A KID LIKE JAKE
Daniel Pearle

Dramatic
Greg: thirties

Greg and his wife Alex are eager to get their son Jake into kindergarten at a top private school. Jake is very bright but lately has started acting out at home and on his school visits, where he's been teased for his gender-nonconforming behavior. Greg is talking to Judy, the head mistress of Jake's pre-school, who has been advising Greg and Alex throughout the process.

GREG: We had a bit of a meltdown. Last week. *(Pause)* Jake wanted to be Snow White for Halloween. And I had said, you know, we could talk about it. But Alex felt strongly it was a bad idea. She's obviously fine with his wearing anything, you know, around the apartment but she was convinced letting him trick-or-treat like that— in the building . . . That neighbors might look at him funny. And she's right that he's observant. And sensitive. Anyway, we'd kinda been delaying the conversation and Halloween rolls around and Alex has a pirate outfit and a skeleton costume laid out for him on his bed and he asks, what about Snow White? And she tells him she doesn't have a Snow White costume but she has these other costumes, and he says he doesn't like these other costumes. And she tries to explain, you know, sometimes you can't have exactly what you want but that's why we have to compromise. And he starts throwing a tantrum. Says he doesn't want to be a skeleton, that her ideas are *lazy*, "*lazy* ideas"—who knows where he— . . . Eventually she said if he wouldn't stop behaving this way he wouldn't be allowed to go trick-or-treating at all and that really sent him over the edge. Screaming at her. "You *lied* to me . . . You're not my *boss*. Daddy said I could." And I kept explaining I hadn't actually said yes but at that point . . . I mean the two of them were really getting into it. She said he was being a baby, that he didn't deserve a costume at all. And he said . . . you know, "You're the worst mom in the entire world and I wish you were *dead* . . . "

(He half-laughs, a little embarrassed.)

Alex thinks maybe we give in too much. He's got all these interviews happening and they're obviously not on his terms and she feels like we owe it to him to set clearer boundaries at home. So he can learn a little more . . . self-control. I don't know. I do worry that he's a little—spoiled. I mean he's an only child, he's got Alex around all the time, a lotta kids don't have that, not to mention, you know, his own *playroom.* It used to be an office—that we shared. I never understood why his toys couldn't just live in his—Anyway, all I'm saying is he is accustomed to getting what he wants. So . . . maybe she has a point.

A Seagull in the Hamptons
Emily Mann

Comic
Alex: Nineteen

Alex's mother is a Famous Actress, a fact that he finds infinitely oppressive; particularly as he detests the theatre— well, the kind of theatre his mother loves. Here, he tells this to his uncle, his mother's brother.

ALEX: My mother hates me. I'm 19 years old and a constant reminder to her that she's not 32. Her whole life is the "theatuh!" And she knows I hate the theater. Not pure theater. I don't hate that. I hate her kind of theater! It's so fake! People marching around pretending like they're in some living room. I mean, all they do is talk and they're boring and pathetic and old . . . and they have nothing to say. I mean, who cares, really? The world is falling apart, or worse, the planet is dying! And these people go to the theatre to be entertained by people who are just like them—or even worse, more clueless than they are! And because the producers are so concerned about not offending anybody while they pay their 100 fucking dollars, there is nothing controversial or worthwhile going on. Unless, of course it's from England! Then of course like good colonialists we bow down to their British accents—anything in British accents makes Americans feel inferior, especially in the theater— and we say it's brilliant, even when it's just —pretentious crap or little dramas with tiny little morals posing as great art—or those fucking cheerful musicals! Oh my God! I don't know. The whole New York theatre scene makes me sick. We have to have a new kind of theater, that's all. Something vibrant, and young, and dangerous and alive or, you know what? Just have nothing at all! *Why do we have to have theater*? I mean, I love my mother but she leads such—a stupid life! She dedicates every waking hour to something that just doesn't matter! And you can imagine how utterly revolting it feels to be me! Here I am at all her stupid parties full of celebrities and people who have all won prizes for something or other—you know, it's ridiculous! Pulitzers and Nobels, and book awards, and Oscars and Tonys and all that crap and here I am! I have nothing to say for myself; I can't even understand what they're talking about half the time; and they're all wondering how Maria could have spawned such a pathetic little loser.

Information on this playwright may be found at www.smithandkraus.com. Click on the AUTHORS tab.

A SEAGULL IN THE HAMPTONS
Emily Mann

Seriocomic
Philip: Forties

Philip, a jaded Famous Writer, tells a young girl named Nina who idolizes him that fame is fleeting and that being a writer isn't all that wonderful.

PHILIP: Do you have any idea what . . . obsession is, or compulsion? Well, the truth of the matter is, I'm not in control of my life. I'm obsessed by one thought: the same thought day and night—and that thought is: I should be writing. I should be writing. I should be writing. No matter what I'm doing, I should be writing. I could be having a glass of wine, or fishing, or making love or having dinner, alright? And my mind is telling me to stop doing what I'm doing because I SHOULD BE WRITING! What kind of dream life is that? It's more of a nightmare, don't you think? I can't enjoy my life because I don't allow myself to live it! In fact, I cannibalize it! I see a poor pathetic girl who is drinking herself and smoking herself to death, dressed like a Goth and I don't comfort her or talk to her I take NOTES! That's what I was just doing when I bumped into you. Taking notes about Milly because I might want to use the details of who she is in a short story or a novel someday. I mean, come on! I'm not living. I'm observing living. I am talking to you here and I look up at the sky for a moment and notice the shape of that cloud formation. Hmmm, I think. It's shaped like a grand piano! I should make a note of that, or on the way here I smelled honey-suckle. That would be a great way to evoke a summer day—the too sweet smell of honeysuckle. Oh, this just goes on forever and ever. It drives me fucking crazy. It's like I'm devouring my own life. And I have no real relationships, no real friends. Most of the people I know, know me and hang out with me because I'm famous, at least for the moment. I am sure as soon as I'm out of favor with the critics, they'll drop me and I won't be invited to any more dinner parties or country houses until I'm in favor again—if that happens in my life-time—and I'll be alone with my goddamn compulsion to notate everything everyone says, or looks like and I'll continue to write it all down until the day I die, and then I'll wake up one day and say, "oh, dear. I forgot to live." And it will be over.

Information on this playwright may be found at www.smithandkraus.com. Click on the AUTHORS tab.

AND AWAY WE GO
Terrence McNally

Dramatic
Scott Harrington: Thirties to forties

Scott is the Artistic Director of a theatre company on the rocks, here telling his audience that he has had to cancel the final production of the season, a much-anticipated King Lear.

SCOTT HARRINGTON: Hello. For those of you who have been living under a rock for our past eight seasons, I'm Scott Harrington, company artistic director. Welcome. Great to see so many familiar faces. How are you enjoying our 49th consecutive season? We want to hear from you. Our subscribers are very important to us. So are our sponsors. Tonight's performance is underwritten by the Geraldine Stutz Foundation and the City Department of Cultural Affairs. Are your cell phones off? Your sentencing will be severe: an entire season of your least favorite playwrights. You know who they are. I have a few more announcements.
   (He looks at his notes.)
Actually, no.
   (He makes an obvious transition in his tone and manner.)
A lot of you were looking forward to our last show of the season *King Lear.* So were we, especially our Lear, company veteran and everybody's favorite, John Pick. Well, we've had to cancel it. A play like *Lear* is a little beyond our reach in the current fiscal climate. Not our reach. As the artistic director I would never say that. Nothing has ever been beyond this company's *reach.* Our mean*s*, rather. A great play needs great resources. In *Lear*'s place we will be presenting Samuel Beckett's *Happy Days.* It's a terrific play and a two-hander. The current crisis caught us short. We didn't see it coming. We were too busy making art. I don't think we *wanted*

to see it coming. Anyway, you must be as tired of these speeches as I am. As my 9-year old would say, "It sucks, daddy." Enjoy the *Orestia*. Curtain up! I keep forgetting, we don't have a curtain.

Information on this playwright may be found
at www.smithandkraus.com. Click on the AUTHORS tab.

BASILICA

Mando Alvarado

Dramatic
Father Gill: Late thirties

Father Gill is speaking at the funeral of a woman named Lela, who was killed in a car crash. When he was a teenager, he got Lela pregnant and then left town, to his eternal regret.

FATHER GILL: On this sad day, I know a lot of you are asking yourself, "Why did God take Lela?" Her death feels like it was an unnecessary tragedy. And for her friends, her family, you feel cheated. Like you've been left in the dark. I say to you, consider the candle that will give you the light you need at this time, consider it to be God. It is natural to question God at a time like this. Have no fear in telling—I am not going to do this anymore. I stare into your faces and it disgusts me. You sit there. Nodding your heads. Shedding your tears. Pretending to care. But you did this. You are responsible for this. And if she had allowed to be who she was none of this would have happened. You have created an environment of lies. You are the same pitiful, conniving, small-minded people that I refused to be like. Stuck in your sins, repeating the same cycle over and over because you are afraid to look in the mirror and really face what you've done. And foolishly, you continue to ask for what will never be given. Why can't you see that? God's not here. I've looked for him. Hoping I would find him. But all I found was filth so dirty, no matter how much you covered it, no matter how much you scrubbed it, it would never be clean. The stench is overwhelming. It suffocated Lela. And now, it's suffocating me. So I'm giving you one last chance at this. Stop pretending. NO MORE PRETENDING! You see, I know the truth. I know every dirty little secret about you. You, got cancer but you don't want to admit to your family because you're broke. You, you're gay and your wife doesn't know it. And you, you slept with your niece. And me? I abandon my son because I was too much of a coward to face up to what I did. That was my sin. And for that, I have paid.

BASILICA
Mando Alvarado

Dramatic
Joe: Late thirties

Joe's wife Lela has recently been killed in a car crash. He is at her grave.

JOE: Ah babe, I'm not doing so good. I just feel so . . . I wish I could tell you that I got the strength. But, you know I would be bullshitting. You always had a way of seeing through me. I know. Like that time, I came home. You put me on that stupid Weight Watcher's Diet. Small portions, no fast food. I was still the same waist size since high school. So I came home. You knew I had a Whataburger. But I said, "No babe, I had a salad and one of those meals, like 3 points and shit." And you just looked me. That night, I was asleep and you came in and jumped on top of me, with the receipt. Whataburger with double meat, double cheese, bacon, mayo, lettuce, tomato, whata-size fries, and whatasized coke. Busted. And an apple pie. So busted. I miss you. Babe. What am I gonna do without you? How did I fuck up babe? My whole life. I tried to do right. I just don't get it. I keep thinking I'm gonna wake up and everything's gonna be fine. Be like it was. Tell me to wake up.

Bird in the Hand

Jorge Ignacio Cortiñas

Seriocomic
Felix: Twenty-seven

Felix is a tour guide at Birdland Family Theme Park.

FELIX: Hi and, yeah, welcome to the Flamingo exhibit. These flamingos you see here today are so out of place, so far from their native ecology, that um, they've started dying off. Enjoy them while you can. You may want to take a few pictures before they go extinct. I mean, my father is going to have to pay for my college tuition and you tourists are clearly willing to pay for admission and the birds are going to die eventually so it's not like it's anyone's fault. Every once in a while, and if we're lucky maybe they'll do it today, the flamingos start to squawk. They start running back and forth—you watch them you swear something is about to happen. They say if you see a flock of flamingos flying it looks like fireworks in the daytime—swirls of red and black feathers. I bet that looks amazing. But right in the middle of their loudest squawking—the flamingos stop. It gets so quiet afterwards, you can hear mosquitoes buzzing. Maybe the Flamingos shut up when they remember—oh yeah—our wings are clipped. They could try walking, theoretically they could walk right out of here, but probably they're not sure where they would go. Probably they can't remember where they're from. Who their friends are supposed to be. Any questions?

BIRD IN THE HAND
Jorge Ignacio Cortiñas

Seriocomic
Felix: Twenty-seven

Felix is a tour guide at Birdland Family Theme Park.

FELIX: Right, so: Welcome to the Flamingo exhibit. I'm kinda hung over this morning, so if you could all keep your questions to a minimum that would be great. Sir—there will be no photography allowed today. Put the camera down sir. Thank you. Now most people think Flamingos are born pink. Actually, Flamingos get their color from their food. We feed them these specially engineered food pellets—which contain this pigment that they used to get from their diet—back in the wild. And for years the food pellets worked. It kept them pink. Eventually though, homesickness catches up with you. Homesickness enters the food chain. And once it's in the food chain, how do you get it out? Specially engineered food pellets don't work anymore. Our staff biologists are working overtime on a permanent cure. Trying to get the pink back. But really, when you think about it, what do scientists know about feeling out of place? About longing? Weird because—actually—I was pretty wasted this morning, and I tried to get a few hours sleep. And I had this dream, where everyone around me speaks a foreign language. And they can't understand what I'm trying to say. I woke up suddenly. And sat up in bed and. I was relieved when I realized the dream wasn't real. And then I laid back down but I couldn't get back to sleep. I was alone and wide-awake and you know—it is real. The loneliness is real.

Bodega Bay
Elisabeth Karlin

Seriocomic
Juan Garza: Early forties, Dominican

Juan is an ex-cop who now makes a living as a private detective. A woman named Louise has hired him to find her mother, who has disappeared. Juan is a big Roberto Clemente fan. He shows Louise a photo of him.

JUAN: You know who that is? That's not some random Pittsburgh Pirate. That's Roberto Clemente! This man was a work of art! He was killed when I was a little kid, before I ever came here. In a plane crash while he was delivering supplies to Nicaragua after the earthquake. You see, it's not for nothing that I won't get on a plane. I like to look at him. It helps me to think. Clemente said that if you don't take the opportunity to help people . . . if you don't do that, then you're wasting your time on this earth.
   (gazing at the picture)
I would marry him if he was a woman . . . and alive. Clemente was a man, you know what I'm saying? Not like these players now who are always "in a slump." I mean, what's that? I don't know what you do for a living, but can you tell your boss you can't do your job 'cause you're in a slump? Of course not! A ball player has two things to do—show up for the games and go to the gym. All the people I know go to the gym *after* work, but a player, that's his job. And with what they get paid! I mean these guys now, they are so delicate like little flowers. They get disabled in body parts I never even heard of. Like, what's a strained oblique? What's that shit? It's not like these guys are carrying bricks.

BROKEN FENCES
Steven Simoncic

Dramatic
Hoody: Mid-thirties, African American

Hoody and his fiancee, D, have lived in Garfield Park their whole lives. As the neighborhood gentrifies, their property taxes have increased and they can no longer afford to live in their own home. This is Hoody's recounting of his life and struggle for survival that continues to this very day. This monologue is delivered to the audience.

HOODY: I am invisible. Been invisible all my life. When I was a kid I could go days, weeks without being seen. Throw my hood up over my head, eyes pushed way back deep inside, and poof . . . just disappear. Blend into the street . . . another shadow . . . another shade of black and grey on the stairs by the train. *(Beat)* Started calling me Hoody. Ain't nobody know my real name . . . and that was fine with me 'cause I didn't need one. And I got used to it too . . . being invisible. I could flow like air, life blowing through me like a breeze. Like I wasn't there. And it was tight too 'cause when you young and you angry and you invisible, you can fuck with people and they don't even know what hit 'em. Can't catch what you can't see. And for a long time ain't nobody see me. Randolph and Kedzie, 1999. I'm standing on the corner, watchin' the Camden projects burn. Marz come running out the house all jacked up, snappin' on this light skinned boy from Pilsen. I'm like 'yo Marz, chill your shit—wasn't the first time my brother's mouth got his ass in trouble— but then this light skinned boy from Pilsen pulls out his nine mil acting all gansta and shit and—POP! POP! Busts two caps just like that. *(Beat)* Marz ran. Didn't look back. Didn't get a scratch. Me . . . I musta been real invisible that day 'cause that boy from Pilsen never even saw me. Bullet passed through me like a pit bull, clawing and scratching and biting its way out. Woke up in Cook County Hospital with a red Bulls jersey *that used to be white* packed into my chest. Don't even know how it got there. *(almost proud)* That was the day I became a little more . . . in focus. The lights come up a bit so we get a better look at his face. After a while I realized the scars weren't just on me, *they were me*. And every year, I got more. Earned every cut, every burn, every bruise, and every tattoo . . . the more marked up I got, the more I could be *seen*. 22. At least here in Garfield Park you ain't had to look hard to see me—*I was everywhere, man*—just connect my dots *(pointing to scars on his arm)* and you got me. *(Beat)* Least the old me. The fuck you me. The *used-to-be* me. Now my shit's retired like MJ. Ham sandwiches and double shifts, that's all I'm pulling these days. Shit I go to Costco. And I *like* it. *(Beat)* Scars are fading . . . dots are disappearing . . . trade your bruise and tattoo for some comfortable shoes . . . and you're left with a whole lot less connect.

Information on this playwright may be found
at www.smithandkraus.com. Click on the AUTHORS tab.

BRONX BOMBERS
Eric Simonson

Dramatic
Reggie: Mid-thirties, African American

Reggie Jackson thinks he has been unappreciated since he signed with the NY Yankees, when he announced that he was going to be "the straw that stirs the drink." His manager Billy Martin, teammate Thurman Munson and Yankee great Yogi Berra have been trying to get him to see himself as part of a team, part of the great Yankee Tradition, which means doing what Martin tells him to do. He responds.

REGGIE: Why?! Why do I gotta do that?! Why do I gotta do anything you tell me? But then I do. I do everything you tell me to. I ride the bus that I *hate*, I room with guys who hate *me*, I play when you say play, and I ride the bench when you say don't, even though the fans want to see me and it makes no sense whatsoever. I keep quiet—I keep quiet and I do what I'm told. And I will continue to do that all year long, and I won't ask to be traded cause that's what I agree to do, and thank *God* Almighty that I am a *good*, Christian, Man! That's right. Jesus! Jesus Christ got my mind right! and he hears my *suffering*! He hears my *prayers*!
(*He drops to his knees.*)
It makes me cry, the way I'm treated on this team. The Yankees are Ruth and DiMaggio and Mantle and Gehrig. I'm a nigger to you, and I just don't know how to be no Elston Howard. I'm making seven-hundred thousand dollars a year, I drive a Rolls Royce and I got homes on both ends of this great country and you treat me like dirt. I've got an I.Q. of one-hundred-sixty, and you can't mess me because you've *never* seen anything like me, and you sure as hell never had anyone like me on the Yankees. I won't fight you, Billy Martin! I'll do whatever you tell me to do on the field, because that is

my contract with you, but you can*not* make me give up on myself! You can*not* make me give up on *me*! See you at the ballpark.

BUZZER

Tracey Scott Wilson

Dramatic
Don: Twenties

Don, who is white, is a recovering drug addict, talking to a group of students at a school in the black neighborhood where he used to buy drugs.

DON: Drugs are really bad news. Why should you listen to me? Seriously. I wouldn't listen to me. I came here as a joke. I mean, Miss Schaffer asked me to come talk to you so I'm here. But I mean who am I? A white guy telling you not to do something. A super, cool white guy but . . . still . . . *(Pause)* I know that you guys are going to do what you're going to do. I can't stop you. Nobody can. I can only tell you what I know. It's fun at first. Great fun. And then suddenly it isn't. Suddenly it's just . . . work. *(Beat)* I've seen some terrible things. I've seen some really brilliant people die and destroy themselves. I almost destroyed myself. But you know, I got a second chance cause my daddy's rich and he got me out of trouble. A lot. But you guys. You don't have that advantage. If any of you guys do half of what I did you will die or be in jail for life. It's not fair, but that's the way it is. I'm lucky. I know that. But you won't be so lucky so why mess up your life? It's not worth it. It's hard to see now but, trust me on this. Get high for a few hours a day, then the next, then you wake up and ten years have passed. And you can't get it back. Ever. It's gone. And all you have left is regret.

CATCH THE FISH
Jonathan Caren

Dramatic
Jordan: Twenty-one

Jordan is at a club in Los Angeles where he's met a woman named Allison who says she's in L.A. for an article she is writing about the scene there. He's hitting it off pretty well with her, even though she's 15 years older than him, and decides to tell her about how he's in deep trouble for something that happened at college.

JORDAN: You won't print a word about what I'm gonna tell you? I'm in college . . . at Michigan . . . It's my third year there and they finally let me pledge a frat. There's this girl Alexis, who I've been hanging out with since the first day in the dorms. I'm basically wanting to be with her but her sorority won't let that happen until I'm a part of Phi Kappa Gamma. Anyway, it's pledge week and they're making us do ridiculous things like sit in a bathtub of raw meat. The week ends with a coed game of capture the flag where whoever gets pegged won't make it into the frat. Me and Alexis, we make a pact not to hit each other so I'm not seeing it coming, but as I'm capturing the flag she comes from behind and smacks me in the head with a water balloon and *breaks our pact.* Now I admit, I kind of lost my shit. So I go to attack her with a hose, but the hose isn't working, so I kind of grab her, playfully, sort of and tackle her to the grass but I accidentally rip her shirt as I'm falling and I hold onto it to keep my balance but the whole thing rips right off of her. Of course I apologize, but she goes ballistic, crying and screaming. The next day I'm being summoned by the Committee for Sexual Misconduct. There were scratches and bruises on her neck and they're treating it like a rape case! I try to talk to her, she won't take my calls. I try to get my boys in as witnesses to back me but nobody would take a stand. They're saying they're going to kick me out of school for that. Luckily, Grant's dad hooks it up and they me finish the semester at a sister program in DC. His dad has pull in the courts and at the schools. Please. Don't say anything. If it wasn't for him, I wouldn't be here right now.

Information on this playwright may be found at www.smithandkraus.com. Click on the AUTHORS tab.

DETAILS
David L. Epstein

Dramatic
Larry: Forty

Unhappy Larry owns a theater company in New York City and has fallen in love with his young assistant. Unable to contain his feelings, he convinces her to go for lunch at a cozy spot in the East Village so he can confess them to her.

LARRY: Do you remember the day we met? You came to interview and the coffee shop was so crowded that we went to the Starbucks across the street. Do you remember that? Remember your white turtleneck, cashmere, three quarters? That's what you wore. I remember every detail of my time with you. What you wear. What you say. How you say it. I study each gesture on your face and the impressions stay with me until it hurts. I remember your three in the morning stories about your collection of leather boots you kept in your college dorm. How you put wine bottles inside of them to keep them propped up? I can tell you the song that was playing the night on the patio when we kissed. Why do you think I show up there at all? Because of you. Because I can be close to you. I don't run around. I've been a devoted husband. But with you, the rules don't apply because I've never felt like this about anyone. You're the girl I want to give everything to. You're the woman I stopped searching for ten years ago.

EXQUISITE POTENTIAL
Stephen Kaplan

Comic
Gary: Thirties

Gary, a rabbi, is talking to a couple who are members of his congregation, Laura and Alan Zuckerman. Alan believes that their 3 year old son David is the Messiah. Gary is trying to disabuse him of that notion.

GARY: Can I tell you a story? A quick one. About a group of monks who lived in a monastery and the monastery was dying. No new monks coming on board. Nobody visited the monastery anymore. A rabbi lived nearby and the monks decided to go to the rabbi and ask him what to do. Anyway, the rabbi knew the story of their failing monastery and told them that one of them was the Messiah and that they should not give up hope. The monks went back home and mulled over what the rabbi had said. The first monk, Monk Larry, thought, "Maybe it's Monk Joe? He's a bit of a grump, but always knows how to say the right thing to somebody." And Monk Joe thought, "What about Monk Larry? When he plays the organ, it's heavenly and always calms everybody's soul." So Monk Joe and Monk Larry started treating each other like the Messiah and things began to change around the monastery. And people began to hear about this monastery and how amazing a place it was. And people began signing up to be monks and visited there and, sure enough, the rabbi was right. Their monastery was saved because each one began to think of the other as the Messiah. It changed their world. Wouldn't it be wonderful if every parent started treating their child as the Messiah? If every parent on Earth, regardless of race, creed, religion—thought that their child was extraordinary? What would the world look like if every kid believed that they had exquisite potential? Wouldn't that truly bring about a Messianic Age?

Fetch Clay, Make Man
Will Power

Dramatic
William Fox: Fifty

Fox, the head of Fox Movie Tone studio, is negotiating the terms of a studio contract with a Negro comedian named Lincoln Perry, better known to us under his nom de plume "Stepin Fetchit," one of the terms of which is that Perry always behave in public, particularly when he is talking to the press, as the phlegmatic, slow-witted man he plays in films, even though Perry was in fact a cultured, educated man.

WILLIAM FOX: No no no, look I know your real name. But to the world you are Stepin Fetchit. Now and forever. It's true. You're Stepin Fetchit. And when you talk like this in the New York Times, speaking of your fondness for concert recitals, Step you confuse the people, and then they hesitate with their money see. And we don't want that do we? No we don't. We want the Fox audiences to be confident, assured, and happy they're going to the picture show to be with their old friend Stepin Fetchit. That puts money in the pockets, and that's what's important. So please stop complaining and do it, that'll be all Step. Oh come on, you're not the only slick one around here. You play a character, I play a character. My character is William Fox, the big man on top of the world here at Fox Movie Tone. And all this, the suits, my cigars, it's all an act. When we came here from Hungary, my family had nothing, Step. And my father continued to have nothing until the day he died-nothing. And there we were, my mother and me, the oldest of 6 children, living in the worst dilapidated East Side tenement you can imagine. It was one of those places where the only water in the building was a shared pump downstairs. We lived on the 5th floor, you get me Step? I had to carry those buckets of water up that rickety staircase day in and day out. One night I had two buckets, and I was rounding the bend that the stairway made from the 4th floor to the 5th, when I lost my balance and all the water came pouring out. I turned to go back down and fetch some more when it hit me, hard smack in the brain. This is my father's life, carrying water up five flights of stairs, spilling it, going back down to get more, carrying it up again, spilling it again, over and over. Do you understand what I'm saying to you? My father, he never advanced, never got ahead no matter how much hard work he did, he couldn't escape who he was. Well, I decided right then and there on those muddy steps that I would play it different, play it cool, I'd become white. And it's the best thing that ever happened to me. Because now I have everything, everything! But do I miss being me sometimes? Sure. Would I trade the new me for the old me? Not on your life. Trust me, it's better on this side. And isn't that why you and I came to Hollywood in the first place? Huh? It's like we're all in one big movie out here, and as long as you play your part, we can all get rich. That's why I love this town. Where else can you make yourself into anything you want?

Information on this playwright may be found at www.smithandkraus.com. Click on the AUTHORS tab.

FETCH CLAY, MAKE MAN
Will Power

Comic
Muhammad Ali: Mid-twenties

Muhammad Ali, who has just changed his name from Cassius Clay, is about to fight Sonny Liston for the second time. He has brought into his entourage the old time movie comedian Lincoln Perry, better known as "Stepin Fetchit," who has suggested that John Ford would be the perfect director for a movie about Ali's life.

MUHAMMAD ALI: Well, I like a Western as much as the next guy, but I just can't see it for my story, no we got to get a brother in the Nation to do it. If you sayin' you concerned about how The White Man bends the way I look and what I say on television, well what's to say John Ford wouldn't do the same thing? He ain't one a us, and no tellin' what he might do, damn he might have me gettin' beat up by some old cowboy or something. Now what would my fans say if they go to the movies and see me, the greatest of all times, gettin' beat up by some cowboy. I mean I wouldn't mind if I lost to the mummy or something like that, 'cause they got supernatural powers. Plus the Mummy is from Egypt, and Egypt is in Africa, which means the Mummy is a brother you dig? And if I gotta get knocked out, I'd rather lose to a supernatural brother than a raggedy old cowboy. Man I could see it now, the new Black man vs. the old Black man. And then at the end, right as we about to get it on, we realize that despite our differences, we one in the same. Only thing is he wrapped up in all them bandages and you can still see me pretty, but besides that we both the same, two black men, and me and the mummy join in the struggle together. Now that would be a movie.

Information on this playwright may be found at www.smithandkraus.com. Click on the AUTHORS tab.

FIRST CLASS
David L. Epstein

Seriocomic
Martin: Thirty

Martin is a photographer being interviewed by a prestigious art gallery curator in Soho. When asked why his images of modern architecture should be on display, this is his response.

MARTIN: When you board an airplane, why do they force everyone to walk through first class? You ever ask yourself? You see, we're forced through first class to make first class passengers feel good about being in first class. I mean, why does first class board first? Wouldn't it make the most sense to board first class last, filling the plane back to front so the most savvy customers spend the least time on board the germ infected plane? I mean, they fill business class back to front, but not first class? No. First class comes on first, they settle in, they hand out lollipops, and although they say they're simply paying for the comfort of wider seats and a better meal, what they really want is the experience of watching the rest of us grow green with envy as we make our way to the back. Now, you look at any new residential building coming up in New York today and you'll see the same hierarchy playing out: You've got the first ten floors all the same, like business class. Then you've got the first class—top of the line penthouse, complete with multiple balconies, gardens, walls made of sheer glass allowing anyone with a high powered lens to peer right in. And why have such big windows? So the rest of the world can grow green with envy when they are able to see with their own eyes how the other half lives.

FIVE MILE LAKE

Rachael Bonds

Seriocomic
Rufus: Mid to late twenties

Rufus tells his friend Jason about Peta, his new girlfriend, who cold-cocked a guy in a bar the night he met her.

RUFUS: So then *he—he* then tries to *recover* and pretends that he DIDN'T say what he just said, like tries to coast over it *entirely*—and she's standing there with like, mouth agape, like—"what the fuuuuuuck did you just say?"—and he's like fumbling around saying like, "well anyway what I meant was, see what I'm trying to say is blah blah" and while he's like shitting his pants she just like—ohmygod—she just *rears back* and—
(He gestures a sucker punch.)
WHAM! She just rears back and punches the guy right in the face. And then like the whole room goes quiet and he's clutching his face and making this *weird* whimpering sound and everyone's staring at him, except for me—because I'm looking at *her*—and you can barely see it, like it's barely there, it's just this tiny, tiny, tiny thing, but I see it. She has this subtle, little snarl going on. Like her lip is slightly curved up on one side—it's really small, like almost imperceptible—but it's there—this like real *animal* thing. And that's it, then I'm just like "I must know this girl. This girl must be in my daily life from now on." Just . . . I mean she really beat the shit out of him. And then that little *snarl.* How do you not walk across the room and immediately introduce yourself to that girl?

FOURTEEN HUNDRED AND SIXTY
SKECTHES OF YOUR LEFT HAND
Duncan Pflaster

Dramatic
Alonso: Twenty, Latino

Alonso is a young painter with Temporal Lobe Epilepsy. He is speaking to his art school friend Paul, on whom he's had a huge crush. Paul has come to stay for the summer with Alonso and his sister Blanca, who has enlisted Paul to keep Alonso taking his medication.

ALONSO: Look, taking the pills dampens everything down for me. It's like wearing a blindfold made of a black and white movie. I can't do it. There's that Leonard Cohen line: "There is a crack in everything. That's how the light gets in." The broken part is where the art comes from. I can't paint, I can't do it, I can't do anything right when I'm on these fucking pills. People didn't have these pills in olden times. Like they didn't have dentists. And they were fine. All my life I've been told I had a special gift. That my art was something magical. I liked it, I wanted to be special. A brilliant tortured artist. Right? We all fall for that image. But then I went to college and met you and bunch of other tortured artists, and we were all special. I mean, you remember Lenny, with his fauvist style? All those bright colors just exploding everywhere. And Sarah's intricate line work, so tight and controlled. How could I compete with Monti, who made me cry once with a painting of Dominick's elbow? And god: and you. We were all the gifted children wherever we came from, and I had no idea how to cope once I got in with everyone who was just as talented and special and stressed just like me. I had to up my game. And then I realized that this talent, this weirdness I have of seeing things a different way, that's what really makes me special. I don't see things like anyone else, so I don't paint like anyone else. I am unique. Without my fucked up brain, what am I? We're shooting stars, that's all we are. Burn brightly, then fade away. Wouldn't you give your life up if it meant that you could be the genius you always knew you were? And you are a genius, my friend; don't be bashful, you know that. If someone was going to take that away, but let you live forever, would you take that bargain?

FOURTEEN HUNDRED AND SIXTY
SKECTHES OF YOUR LEFT HAND
Duncan Pflaster

Seriocomic
Gabriel: Thirty-two

Gabriel is a soldier who's come to propose to his girlfriend Blanca while on leave from the Army. Unbeknownst to him, she's been having an affair with a painter named Paul, who's staying with her brother Alonso and her for the summer. When Gabriel arrives, Paul manipulates him into posing nude for him and Alonso. Gabriel speaks to the audience as his inner monologue during the painting session.

GABRIEL: Yeah, I know I've got a good body. I work out. And God blessed me with a pretty good dick. It does what I need it to, when I want it to. Girls are usually impressed. And I've never had any complaints. And you know, part of having a nice body, part of working to have a nice body, is that you want people to look. You want people to check out the merchandise and approve. But this shit is different. I mean, not because Alonso and Paul are dudes, other dudes check me out all the time, and it's like whatever, jealous guys who want to be me, or homos checking me out in the gym who wish they could get up on this, you know. I let 'em look. I'm a man. Or, you know, showering with other dudes in the army, you sometimes have to see other guys briefly out of the corner of your eye, just when they end up in your periphery. Or pranks. There's nothing funnier than getting some poor bastard friend of yours stripped and humiliated. I mean, we're way beyond just sharpieing a dick on a bro's face. That's amateur. We make an art out of it. We totally got Danny a few days before I left, got him completely wasted: he woke up naked, painted blue except for his little dick and with an American flag stuck in his ass. And last month poor Scotty passed out drunk and got tea-bagged by the entire barracks; there's video up on YouTube, it's a private link, but we've all seen it. Even I've got pranked a couple of times. Once I woke up bare-ass 12-50 naked, Saran-wrapped to my buddy Adam. Who was also naked. And they cracked some eggs on us. And Adam got Scott's dick rubbed on his face as revenge for the tea-bagging. There were so many pictures of that shit. It's just guys having fun, and when it's all guys, you get to know what you all look like naked. It's a status thing. If you can get your buddy to acknowledge that you're superior, you win. It's just part of being a man, right? So I am totally cool with being seen without clothes on. But this is different. Actually sitting. Voluntarily. Inviting them to look. Naw, they're not just looking, they're studying me. I've never had anyone just stare at my body for this long. This is kind of uncomfortable. You done drawing my dick yet?

GEORGIE GETS A FACELIFT
Daniel Guyton

Dramatic
Georgie: Twenties

Georgie is a troubled man. He has just killed a girl scout by accident, to whose body he addresses this monologue.

GEORGIE: Let me tell you a *lesson* about *life*! Ok? Life is not . . . What do you do? You sell Girl Scout cookies? Ok, let me tell you something. What do you gotta sell? Like 300 of them? Ok. Let's just say you gotta sell, like, 300 Thin Mints, ok? Like you got, ok, you got, like, 300 *boxes* of Thin Mints, right? Ok, you got 300 boxes of Thin Mints because those are the *cookies* that everybody loves, right? Ok, so here you are, you're sellin 'em. "Whoop de doo! Buy my Thin Mints!" Right? So, what happens? You sell 300 Thin Mints and what do you get? A medal? A fuckin *patch* on your shawl that says "Look at *me*, I sold three-hundred *boxes* of THIN MINTS?!?" Is that what it's *for*? A fucking PATCH?!?
(He calms down.)
Well, that's cool. Because I mean, you know, patches are nice. They add a little color, a little . . . flavor to your brown and green. But . . . you just don't *understand*. You just don't under*stand* that for every *patch* you receive in life, there will be some motherfucker ready to stab you in the back and steal your patch *away* from you!!! You just don't understand this.
(He cries.)
And I'm teaching you a lesson. There will be some mother . . . You just don't understand. You're just a little girl. *(Pause)* I had a patch, too, once. You think I'm a monster, but I had a patch, *too*. It was called a Bachelor's Degree. I thought, "I could own the world."

Spent six years in college and I thought, "Man, I finally got it right." Spent six years in . . . I finally got it right. I thought, "Now I can get a job. Now I can do something with my life." You think I'm a monster. You think I'm a monster 'cause I shot you, don't you? You think . . . Well, I'm not a monster. I only did it 'cause I care. I only did it 'cause . . .

(He stands.)

You're right, I *am* a monster. They took my *job* away! What else could I do? I spent six years in *college* and they took my *job* away! I . . . What else could I *do*? They stabbed me in the back and took my job away. Just one mistake and they never let it die. Just . . . one mistake. And they *never* let it die. I just want my patch.

GOOD TELEVISION
Rod McLachlan

Seriocomic
Mackson: Twenty-three

Mackson is talking to Connie, a TV producer who does a "reality show" about addiction which involves a family coping with the addiction of one of their members and his rehab. Machson wants to participate in the show. Clemmy (short for Clemson) is his brother and is a crystal meth addict. Brittany is his sister.

MACKSON: Hey, you mind if I ask you, I watch your show, its fantastic, really good television. Can I ask you, that drug addict treatment is really expensive, right? So you got that in your budget? You pay for all that rehab, what you got maybe . . . well, some of your shows got two addicts, some just one . . . so lets say eighteen addicts a season times a hundred thousand dollars . . . Cause, I was gonna say, that's like almost two million dollars . . . Well, its a gift for you . . . for the addict its sort of like selling their life rights, really. Innit? The rehab joint gets their plug, Clemmy gets your super dooper rehab, in return for lettin' you show the whole world he's toothless and all messed up. Its like he sold his life rights to you, but instead of money he gets detox. But for you guys, all that rehab you're offerin' is pure gift. *(Pause)* Which is fair. I love the show, I love what ya'll do. I was the one that made that audition tape happen, you know. I showed Brit how to use the camera, and I coached 'em. Just on how to do the tape. Just what the tape is supposed to be.
    (Beat)
I wanna say, seriously, I'm ready to do my part. I feel bad about all this. I knew I wasn't really helping enough. Everything fell apart for Clemmy and Brit when Daddy flew the coop. I was twenty-two and wanted to get myself started in my career. Was I . . . was I selfish? Brittany

thinks I was. Maybe she's right. So fuck it, I did leave 'em in the lurch and now I intend to use my knowledge to help my family out. And, sure, I would certainly appreciate your help. If you can get him all this expensive rehab and interventions and all this, hey, I'm on the team. Hundred per cent.

Information on this playwright may be found at www.smithandkraus.com. Click on the AUTHORS tab.

GOOD TELEVISION
Rod McLachlan

Dramatic
Ethan: Thirty-three

Ethan is the director of a reality TV show about addict, their rehabilitation, and their families. He is laying into Connie, the producer. Because of her, an episode got screwed up.

ETHAN: I knew exactly what to do. I SHOT it. But because things got a little messy, not according to your perfect world recovery script, we lost the episode and a chance to do some good for the MacAddys. I think you of all people should see the problem with that. I know you've had your own struggle with addiction . . . And I know that you lost some addicts in the past, and that's got to be tough . . . and I bet you're honest enough to admit that there's a tendency among addictive personalities to view everything in black and white terms. I don't think I need a degree to see you've got some issues you're not willing to face. You all talk about being documentary. Is it really documentary if your recovery rate is seventy per cent? Is that showing the truth? Or just making sure everyone feels heroic and non-exploitative? I understand now how painful it is to see an addict fail. So it makes sense you've convinced yourself, and everyone else here, that to be compelling television every episode needs an up ending. But in fact, showing the truth is compelling television. The *reality* of it . . . no matter what the ending is. So whether Clemmy got a by-the-book intervention or not, I think we could have convinced him to finish our show and offered him treatment at a decent center. BUT, if he still said no, I'd shoot that. Because our show *is* documentary. And there might be failures, not because our schedule is tight, but because our show is about drug addicts. And drunks. And anorexics. We make documentaries about people trying to die. Your choice of subjects, that wasn't about making good television, it was about you protecting your comfort level.

Information on this playwright may be found at www.smithandkraus.com. Click on the AUTHORS tab

H20

Jane Martin

Dramatic
Jake: Late thirties

Jake is the star of the Dreamwalker *action movie series. He never acted before, and now he's famous, and can do anything he wants. He is directing a production of* Hamlet. *He is speaking to Deborah, an actress who is a committed Christian, who saved him when he tried to commit suicide and who he wants to play Ophelia.*

JAKE: Dawnwalker is an ordinary cabdriver born without a tongue who discovered his superpowers and destroys legions of incubi and succubi from hell running an international monetary scam thus making Dreamworks hundreds of millions of dollars and thus a god who can change at will the opening date of a limited run of *Hamlet* on Broadway. And just to warn you, I am crazy. My mom said I was crazy, my teachers said I was crazy, Louisa said I was crazy, the army said I was crazy, three psychotherapists said I was crazy and I say I'm crazy. There's an incredible amount of stuff I can't make sense of, myself as one example, so I get drawn to stuff that I instinctually think makes sense even if I can't explain it and the most recent example would be you. Now you should drink your ginger-lemonade before the ice melts. Acting, for instance, is senseless. Why? What intrinsic value does it have? For people who watch it, it works in the same way as miniature golf. It's one of a hundred distractions that get us through a meaningless landscape. But I recognize Shakespeare is a different deal. He knows something and out of this mysterious knowledge he makes poetry that kills. So I thought I would attach my meaningless self to his meaningful self and see if it worked like a transfusion.

(She starts to speak.)

Wait. But, see, I'm terrified. I read the play and my hands shake. But because I'm crazy, I have this instinct, this blind drive that tells me that the play will clean me like a hot shower, that I will go out there night after night, consider suicide and reject it as dishonorable, and I have a Jones for honor.

(She starts to speak.)

Wait. But my will is diminished and my fear is great and I need your certainty to get me there. I need somebody with a larger purpose . . . somebody God speaks to, to put some steel in my shaken self, because I can't do this on my own, surrounded by . . . Thespians. Please help me.

Information on this playwright may be found
at www.smithandkraus.com. Click on the AUTHORS tab.

H20

Jane Martin

Dramatic
Jake: Late thirties

Jake, a movie star, is directing and starring in a production of Hamlet *on Broadway, quite a challenge for him as he has never acted on the stage before, nor has he ever directed a play. Here, he is in a bar, drinking himself into a stupor while talking to the bartender.*

JAKE: I can't do this part. Who can do this part? It makes no sense! He won't kill Claudius . . . who has murdered his father by the way . . . because of his religion we gather, but he has to kill him because of his honor, so he agonizes, he agonizes, he agonizes and kills Polonius, which is okay for some reason, flees to England, jumps ship and ends up with pirates, how am I supposed to act pirates, makes it back to Ophelia's funeral, who he drove to suicide, and is, we don't know why, an entirely different guy. Now he wants to kill everybody. Jumps into Ophelia's grave and punches out her brother. What, we might ask, is going on here? He leaves out all the key scenes from 'can't Kill Claudius' to 'Must Kill Claudius' and what the hell kind of writing is that? This is the greatest play ever written? This is the guy who brought psychology to the stage? It's a con game of a play by a playwright who very possibly didn't write it, done for an elderly audience who use it to punish their grandchildren, by snobbish British actors who despise the audience and think an emotion is when you take your voice down half an octave, for critics who invariably say you aren't as good as the guy who played it last year, and because the playwright, having no idea how to end it, just kills everybody! And what is worst of all, insufferable, is that everybody has advice. Everybody. What the hell was I thinking?! What? Bartender, another bottle and a clean glass. Yeah, I was on the floor but I got up.

Information on this playwright may be found at www.smithandkraus.com. Click on the AUTHORS tab.

HARBOR

Chad Beguelin

Dramatic
Ted: Late thirties

*Ted is explaining to his partner Kevin why they can't take
Kevin's screw up of a sister Donna's baby.*

TED: Look, I love you, Kevin. But for all intents and purposes you are not an adult. I know, mathematically you are. Physically? Obviously. But emotionally? You have to be coddled and supported financially, not that I have ever balked at that, not that I didn't suggest it even, but you have to be taken care of. You're needy and dependent and maybe that's what I love about you, because I like to be the one taking care of people. But I get to choose the people, Kevin. Get it? I get to choose the people and I already have my plate full. I'm sorry. Maybe that's not the way it should have come out. But, let's be practical here. Let's just take the financial aspect of this little thing you've agreed to behind my back. I just lost two bids last week. I have frighteningly little income. I had to lay off half of my staff and we still have to pay the mortgage and the electric bill and whatever the hell else we need and now you want to take in a baby and pay for clothes and school and college and whatnot when you aren't even bringing in one red cent. The book. I don't know, it's been ten years and if you were a writer you would, hmmm, let's see, I don't know, maybe write something? Or if not, then realize that that dog won't hunt and take some initiative and temp or learn a trade that you can actually perform. Wait, I didn't mean to say that like that. Wait, I didn't mean to say that like that. I'm just trying to be honest with you, to lay our cards on the table. I am not raising a baby. That's not anything that I want to pursue. So, I don't know what to tell you.

HEARTS LIKE FISTS

Adam Szymkowicz

Dramatic
Peter: Thirties

Peter is talking to the artificial heart he built, but in a presentational way. He has just put his prototype heart into the evil and misunderstood Dr. X, a heart he himself needed. He's talking to the spare.

PETER: Here you are, my spare heart. Mother said, always have a spare. You never know, she said. Do everything twice. Just in case. Always have an extra pencil. Always bring an extra sandwich. And give it away if you can. To the kid with the torn jacket who smells like pee. And if they say thank you, say "you're welcome," or "think nothing of it," or "no thanks is necessary." Tell them "I can see you're a human being who needs something. We all need something sometimes and if I can be the one to help, well that is good, but next time it could be you that helps and that will be good too." Always do what you can to help. And if you think someone is laughing at you, look away. Look away. You'll save them all some day, she said. And now I will. I look to you, artificial heart. I look to you and I hope you know how to beat endlessly like I taught you. Because I'm going to make a million of you, and then another million, and another. Anyone who wants you, can have you. Anyone who feels weak will be made strong by your comforting weight and your life-saving pumping. You will be the circulatory saver of this world. But right now, I'm the one in need of your help. I'm the weak one, the sick, the damaged, the other. I'm the kid with the torn jacket, except the jacket is a heart. Tomorrow, they will crack my chest open and put you inside, and then I will never need to be afraid again.

Information on this playwright may be found
at www.smithandkraus.com. Click on the AUTHORS tab.

HOW WATER BEHAVES
Sherry Kramer

Dramatic
Steve: Mid to late twenties

Steve lost his job and he and his wife Nan are in dire financial straits. They have started a bogus charity and Nan has really gotten into it. She also wants to start a family. Steve, who's become very cynical about the ways of the world, wants out—of the "charity" and their marriage.

STEVE: What did you think? That this was a freebie—a fantasy—that there were no consequences? You wanted to pretend to save the world, and feel good about it, and then go on with your life? No right? I have every right. Why do you think people don't repair the world? Because they're cheap? Because they're lazy? Because they just didn't think of it? You think it's some new idea you had, and now that you're spreading the word, everybody is going to say, "Why didn't I think of that? Now that you've enlightened me, sign me up, I'm on board." No, Nan. People wake up, every day, and they think, "I can repair the world, or I can fix my car. I can repair the world, or send my kid to college." And a couple thousand times, waking up like that, they stop thinking about repairing the world at all. Repairing the world is for rich people, not us. We don't get to do it. They do. It is the ultimate right and privilege of the rich. I'm not saying it's wrong to want to change the world, and make it better. Everybody wants a piece of that. The little people give in dribs and drabs, they race for the cure, they band together, they raise this or that. And they give a bigger percentage of their worth to charity than the rich, everywhere on earth. But they could give it all, and it wouldn't matter. Grow up, Nan. There are people in America with more wealth than entire countries. You know how every country changes the course of its rivers, sooner or later? To make dams or to control flooding or just for the fucking sheer hell of it? That's how much money you need to make a difference. You need enough to control the course of the river of money that flows through the world. You need to control that flow. And if you can't do that, then you're just a bobbing cork at the mercy of the current. The reason why people don't repair the world is because they can't afford it. We can't afford it. But we made a pledge to do it anyway. That doesn't mean there isn't a cost. A cost you don't want to pay. But I have to, Nan. Keep living in your fantasy! Keep idolizing Melinda Gates! But guess what? The rich are different from you and me. THEY HAVE MONEY.

I WANNA DESTROY YOU
Joshua Conkel

Comic
Hal: Fifties

Hal explains to a gay friend why he thinks it would be so much easier to be gay than straight.

HAL: People have this glue, see, that makes them stick together. Once you're intimate with somebody, that is. Women have a lot of it. Men have less, and this is why marriage works, see? Because the woman sticks to the man. Now. Two women are intimate and they move in and domesticate almost instantly. The old lesbian u-haul joke. Two men? There's no glue. Nothing to bind them. So . . . they can be intimate and then just move on. Must be fantastic. When I was a young man I had sex with just about any girl that would let me. No matter if they were chunky or a bit cross-eyed or once pooped their pants at Sarah Lawrence. I mean, I got it from all sides. I was so handsome, though of course I didn't know that then. I got syphilis once in Thailand. Crabs a couple of times. And then, when I was about thirty-five or so, I thought perhaps I'd be celibate. I'd sexed myself out. Well. That lasted about thirteen seconds, let me tell you. I realized that making love was how I got to know a woman, see. It was my way of saying, "Hey. Pleased to meet you." And now I'm gonna marry Cecile. One woman. Amazing how we drift into things in life, isn't it? You find yourself some place and you think, "How did I get here? I don't recognize this."
(Beat)
So you wanna marry your friend, huh? Well, that's great. I'm in favor of it, sincerely. I wish you the best, little buddy. I really do.

Information on this playwright may be found at www.smithandkraus.com. Click on the AUTHORS tab.

Just Another Day on Death Row

Joan Forster

Dramatic
Billy: Twenties

Billy, who is in prison on death row, is speaking to a corrections officer while waiting to find out his fate.

BILLY: I don't know. Maybe that's not all I'm scared of . . . I'm all tangled up inside. I'm scared of coming up out of the darkness where it's safe. It's that light of truth I'm scared of . . . the light of truth that tells ya you've wasted your life and it's too late to do anything about it. . . it's like a neon light beatin' you to death when you're already down. But then sometimes I think maybe if you grab onto the light and hold it long enough it'll give you courage . . . maybe it's just that first burst of light that makes you want to run back to the darkness. *(Pause)* I stopped at this gas station once to use the john. And there it was on the wall . . . staring me right in the face . . . the truth shall set you free . . . they ought to print that on every billboard across the country instead of advertising some product for jock itch or deodorant or some shit like that . . . If anything could move the earth under your feet it's those six little words . . .It was like that sayin' was meant for everybody to see . . . no matter who you were . . . whether you drove a big flashy car or walked around with holes in your shoes you had to stop sometime to take a leak, and there it'd be on the wall . . . I never forgot it . . .

Information on this playwright may be found at
www.smithandkraus.com. Click on the AUTHORS tab.

LAST FIRST KISS
Chad Beckim

Dramatic
Peter: Eighteen

Peter's prom date, Gabby, has just seen him kissing another boy, and he is trying to explain, and to console her.

PETER: This isn't going to make much sense to you because this doesn't make much sense to me, but I'm going to say it because if I stop to think about it I might not ever say it. Okay? So just let me talk and then we'll deal with the aftermath. *(takes a breath, begins)* When I was eight, I caught my mom stuffing my Christmas stocking. Caught her red handed, hand in the stocking, assorted trinkets in her other hand, no room for explanation. So at eight? No Santa—he's dead to me. So I know this—fact—there is no Santa. But even after that, even after I knew, I wanted so badly to believe in Santa that I, what, I tricked myself. For another three years I tricked myself. And now? We're here. But that's not all . . . you ready? Here goes . . . I love you, Gabby. I really do. When we started . . . dating . . . I kept thinking that things would, whatever, change and all that. That I would become attracted to who I am supposed to be attracted to. That didn't happen. And I'm sorry for that. But it doesn't change the fact that I love you, in spite of me, because of, because . . . you are the best person I know. The best. There's no denying that. You are the best. And I am sorry, Gab. You have no idea how sorry I am that this happened tonight, of all nights. I never would have planned this, you have to understand that, never in a million years, because that would make me slime. It just happened. You have to believe that. BUT . . . if there were ever going to be someone, a girl—no, a woman . . . it would . . . be you. And I don't mean that in some sort of, cereal box, consolation prize way, but in a way that's as honest as anything I can ever say. If there was? It would be you. Does that make sense?

LEGACIES

Kermit Frazier

Dramatic

Carleton: Twenty-seven, African American

Speaking to his 16-year-old nephew Joseph near a bench in the park, Carleton tells the story of his recently traveling to Washington, DC, to view his older brother's name on the Vietnam Memorial.

CARLETON: I took me a bus trip to D.C. last weekend. Went there to see the Vietnam thing. The memorial. Went by myself. Didn't tell nobody I was goin' 'cause I knew nobody woulda wanted to go with me anyway. It's been almost a year since it was dedicated so like it was about time, you know . . . . But when I got to the Mall, well, I kinda got lost at first. Stumblin' all over the damn Monument grounds. Kept runnin' into all the wrong things. Fuckin' tourists and ducks and ponds and twisy paths and shit. But then finally: *boom*. There it was. Just over this one particular rise. And it was like a shock, you know. All gleaming in the sun. All stone-stiff and swept along the ground like the humongous wings of some damn dead airplane. Nose buried. Tail shot off and gone. And it really ain't all that crowded so I'm feelin' okay, you know. Kinda right, ready . . . . I make my way to one of them books under glass at one of the entrances. Flip through the pages, find Eddie's name. And that sends me to the right panel and line, see. And hey, what do you know? I mean like what do you fuckin' know? Like he's just got to be in the middle, right? Almost stone dead in the middle of the whole goddam thing. And I . . . I get up close, see. Stand right before it. And I read . . . I read: Edward A. Wallace, Jr.

(lifting his right hand)

I lift my right hand and it starts shakin', shakin' like a damn leaf. And somethin' starts turnin' upside down in my guts. But I don't stop

(tracing the air)
'Cause I've gotta do it. I've gotta trace every single letter in my big brother's name. 'Cause I'm hopin' that maybe it'd be over then, finished, all this crazy-assed shit inside of me.
(He stops tracing.)
But it don't work. It don't fuckin' work.
(He lets out a little laugh.)
And you wanna know why? 'Cause all the while I'm doin' it I can fuckin' see myself, man.
(He slowly begins backing US away from "the wall.")
See myself right there in that glassy stone wall. My reflection lookin' back at me lookin' back at those goddam small-assed little chiseled letters.
(He pulls out the knife his brother left him.)
Chiseled.
(He raises the knife to his face and seems to be chiseling letters into his forehead as he speaks.)
Edward A. Wallace, Jr. chiseled right across my own forehead.
(He lowers the knife to his side.)
No escape, Little Joe. No fuckin' escape."

Information on this playwright may be found at www.smithandkraus.com. Click on the AUTHORS tab.

L<small>EGACIES</small>

Kermit Frazier

Dramatic
Franklin: Fifty-three, African American

With half-drunken honesty Franklin reveals to Battles, a fellow college professor and good friend, how at 17 he attempted to get out from under his preacher father's influence only to wind up secretly getting a girl pregnant.

FRANKLIN: *(Softly begins to sing a Baptist Hymn.)*
We are soldiers in the Army.
We've got to fight although we have to cry.
We've got to hold up the bloodstained banner.
We've got to hold it up until we . . .
(He keeps the word "die" to himself.)
The thing is . . . the thing is, see. You've got this powerful preacher of a father who, among other things, writes sermons that'll sear your eyes if you get too close to the pages they're written on. And he's telling you how he wants you to be a preacher just like him 'cause, after all, *his* daddy was a preacher, and you *are* the only son in the family, sandwiched, as it were, between two older sisters and a precious younger sister who's the apple of daddy preacher's eye. And you find yourself almost blindly saying yes, yes, I want to, I need to, I must. It's a part of me, a part of us. And yet all the while some tiny little demon inside you is saying, no, uh-uh, 'cause you're nervous half the time, hesitant, scared. And you begin dreaming about running away, escaping to all the places you read about in novels and stories 'cause for you the world of books, the world of provocative, silently breathing words, is perhaps the most precious of all. . . . And then this girl. This beautiful, fun-loving girl you meet on the street one day. Just by chance. Carlene Humphrey. And for the first time in your life you feel sooo . . . good
(speaking as his father)

You'd better cut that girl loose, boy. Just cut her loose. You're barkin' up the wrong tree. Travelin' in the wrong circles. You've got yourself a name, a reputation. You've got yourself someplace to go. Someplace special! You gotta stay *on* track, not *across* the tracks.

(Pause. Back as himself)

I'm gonna keep seeing her, Battles. Because there's no other way.

Information on this playwright may be found at www.smithandkraus.com. Click on the AUTHORS tab.

Love Sick
Kristina Poe

Dramatic
Chris: Thirty-five

Chris is at a group therapy session for the broken hearted, finally doing his step where he has to state clearly what happened and how he came to be in the group.

CHRIS: *(very uncomfortable)* My name is Chris. I am here, sharing with the group because my wife left me. I feel sad, and lonely, but mostly what I feel is shame. Shame because I was not man enough to hold on to my woman. And I know that sounds caveman-ish, or whatever, but in my heart, I know I am not a real man, because a real man would have been able to keep her. A real man would have satisfied his wife, so she didn't go looking for satisfaction elsewhere. And not just sexual satisfaction either, though that was part of it—but financial and familial is just as important. With me she lived in an apartment . . . with him she lives in a two story house with a pool and four kids . . . ALL boys, even. So, I live with great shame knowing I am not a real man. And other men know I'm not a real man, they have proof, my wife left me. Well, first she cheated on me, and left me, then came back to try and work it out when the affair ended . . . but then, within two months she was cheating on me again, with this Chester White. And then she told me she loved me, but she was leaving me for that guy. And she did . . . and six weeks later she was pregnant. I don't hang out with my guy friends too much anymore, cuz they know. They've been great, but they respect me a little less; I can see it in their eyes. And it hurts. But what really hurts, what is really almost unbearable is the mornings. Because in the mornings, when I wake up, my mind is clear, and fresh, and for a few brief moments, I am the Man I used to be

—happy and with his wife still in love with him . . . but then, at some point, usually about a minute later, my brain kicks on, and I remember that my life has turned upside down, and all of a sudden, I experience that devastation all over again, in full force. And it is crushing. And it's that moment, where I wonder if it's all worth it.

MAD LOVE
Marisa Smith

Comic
Doug: Twenties

Doug has been addled since he jumped out a window during a frat party in college and hit his head, but he still knows a thing or three about women, and here he imparts some of his vast knowledge to his brother Brandon, who can't figure out his on again/off again relationship with his girlfriend, Sloane.

DOUG : I get women, dude, I was born getting women. I mean, people say women are all complicated and mysterious and stuff but that's a lie. That's a big lie. They are simple, man, I mean there are some things that all women like—it doesn't matter how liberated and feminated they are. Like jewelry. There is no woman on the planet who doesn't like jewelry, not one, it's impossible, they are totally hard wired for shiny and sparkly. Or glitter, they are suckers for glitter. Like a great present would be glitter in all kinds of colors. I knew this girl—shit I can't remember her name—she put it in her lady garden and I had glitter on my dick for weeks. I couldn't get those suckers off. And bro, this is something not many people know, this is like secret information. You know what girls really like, like anywhere, anytime? I mean this makes them so happy. Unbelievable happy. I've tried it, it always works. *(pause)* Bubbles. Yeah, bubbles. You go to the toy store and you buy those bubbles that come with a wand and you just blow some and they start laughing and thinking it's so cute. I'm telling you. Bubbles. All chicks like bubbles. They totally love you for it dude. Bubbles.

Information on this playwright may be found at
www.smithandkraus.com. Click on the AUTHORS tab.

MIDDLEMEN

David Jenkins

Seriocomic
Michael: Mid-late twenties

Michael Aaronson is exhausted and his nerves are worn. Normally a truthful and trusting person, he has found himself complicit in the bankrupting of Bolivia, and fears the consequences. This is direct address to the audience.

MICHAEL: I don't sleep. *(Beat)* Not anymore, not lately. *(Beat)* It's not by choice. I *like* sleep, it's not . . . a boycott or anything. *(Beat)* I doze. Can't remember the last time I had a good night's . . . When I used to sleep, I would dream of numbers. Peaceful dreams (I love numbers). I dream of other things, too, but the ones I remember the most vividly are math based. It's just, lately I . . . I haven't been able to shut my mind off. Listen we're all adults here, right? We know that everything . . . you know . . . in *business* . . . operates on a sort of flexibility. We're all adults, we know that. Why should my job be any different? I'm not, uh, not immune to the laws of physics, I know that sometimes you have to make a deficit look like a surplus, or move a decimal point here or there. *(Beat)* You get numbers on their own, in their natural habitat, and they're fine. But you put them in the hands of human beings . . . Things Mean Things. You know? *(Beat)* I know I'm being vague. Uh, coffee cup here *(picking up a mug)* will always mean coffee cup. You can smash it, and it turns into porcelain shards, or smash it further until it's just dust, but as long as it's in this form, this will always equal coffee cup. It doesn't equal cat, or car. Do you, do you know . . . ? (Okay, just bear with me here. This sort of thing might be why I'm still single.) Uh, all through our lives, all around us, we have these, uh, *facts*, I guess. This is my hand, not my foot. Okay, check, I know that, I'm never going to have to be reminded of that again, I can go on with my life, and never doubt that information. And that's numbers. These are *things* . . . they're . . . they're *facts*. And I'm in the position a lot of times of being asked to say that a coffee cup is a cat, and, and, I . . . . Long story short, I may have bankrupted Bolivia.

Information on this playwright may be found at www.smithandkraus.com. Click on the AUTHORS tab.

MIDDLEMEN
David Jenkins

Seriocomic
Stan: fifties

Stan and his young co-worker Michael are both somewhat complicit in the bankrupting of Bolivia, and Stan attempts to talk Michael out of confessing to the authorities.

STAN: You. Are not. Special. *(Beat)* You are not important. I know, your parents told you differently, but they were lying. If you were never born, if you had never existed at all, this exact same thing would have happened— and I'm not saying that it did—in *exactly* the same way. *(Beat)* That applies to me, too. We are just not that impor . . . Don't do this, don't go down this alley. We didn't get to be the—I'm going to spoil it for you Mike—we didn't get to be the big fish. We're never going to be . . . I mean, we're not the bottom, and that's, you know, that's good. But we're not destined to be the top of the . . . We're somewhere in between. *(Beat)* And there's comfort to be taken in that Michael, because there's more of us, and there's safety in numbers. You ever see a school of fish? You see how they all turn at the same time? *(Beat)* How do they know? When to turn? This is us. *(Beat)* We turn, and then we swim, and we turn again, and then we eat some seaweed and we call it a day. And that's okay, that can be okay. Because when the . . . hits the . . . we're not the ones who end up . . . little fish make terrible trophies, Michael. You don't want a minnow on your wall, you want a great big tuna fish. With their great big cars and houses and their wives . . . with all the hair . . . and the great big diamond rings. Those are the guys you want to nail, if you're looking to nail someone, the big guys, with the offices, and the jets. No one is going to make their name sending you to the slammer. Or me. We're not worth the . . . *(Beat)* You are piss, Michael, in the ocean, essentially. If something went awry, there's bigger fish to fry than you. *(Beat)* Do you feel better?

Information on this playwright may be found at
www.smithandkraus.com. Click on the AUTHORS tab.

MODERN PROPHET
Sam Graber

Dramatic
Eli: Forties, African American

The ancient biblical prophet Elijah has run away from God. He is welcomed into a Minnesota cabin by a woman who has been abducted by her energy-scavenging husband. Eli is lost and weary and burdened.

ELI: All I hear is laughter. I rejected humanity and God laughed at me. When you reject humanity God will laugh at you. That was the problem, this man in the story, believing God and not believing in His people. The first time this man was provided the sight, the first time that the visions came through glass and stars, the man turned over himself to God's will. Zealot in chief! And not for humanity, not for God's creatures, because what's the point of scurrying with the weakness when you've been bound to the strength. And this man fought, he toiled for that God, to face the Queen corrupter, only to be told by that God to go and hide. Get thee to the cave. And by that cave the fire came first, then the winds of hurricane, but God was barely there, now a small voice, just a small voice, and this man knew he was alone. This man couldn't believe it, how someone could serve with such utter and relentless devotion and get turned out, abandoned by the very God he was serving. Well. The man never died. The man wasn't allowed to die. He was condemned. To sit in his chair while fathers carve up their boys, to drink from his cup at every remembrance, to serve as witness to humanity's unending adherence to God simply because this man didn't believe it was possible. You sit in enough chairs and drink from enough cups and you have time to think. Obedience to God isn't the message. The message is obedience to each other. And it just takes one mistake, and God will laugh at you.

Information on this playwright may be found at www.smithandkraus.com. Click on the AUTHORS tab.

NIGHTNIGHT

Lucas Hnath

Dramatic
Tom: Twenties to Thirties

Tom is an astronaut on a space shuttle, here describing a terrible recurring dream.

TOM: I sleep all night now, but when I sleep, it's all nightmares. Terrible nightmares, nightmares about the space walk. Every night, same nightmare, where I'm out there in the suit and the tether breaks. In the dream, I never see how it breaks or why it breaks, but that's what happens, every time: the tether breaks, and I try to grab onto the edge of the ship but I miss and I just keep going farther and farther away from the space craft. And my suit is equipped with a nitrogen blast. And I fire it and hope that it sends me back in the direction of the space craft. But every time it either doesn't fire or it misfires or it fires but it fires in the wrong direction. And so I keep floating because there's nothing to stop me. But I have my radio, and I have about 45 minutes of oxygen left in my primary tank, and I can hear mission control and they can hear me. and the people on earth, in mission control, they can patch me through to maybe a girlfriend or something. And I try calling but she doesn't pick up. So I try calling one of the other girlfriends, but she's not home. And I ask mission control to play me a song or something, but in the dream, they don't have any of the music that I like, and so I sit in silence and look around and I can see the stars, and the stars look different because all I have is a thin visor between me and the stars and I can see what starlight really looks like and real starlight is all sorts of colors like red and purple and blue. And when my 45 minutes of oxygen run out, I have a choice: I can let them run out or I can switch to my secondary tank, and that will give my another 2 hours and I can use that extra time to call my mother and say goodbye or I could just keep drifting off and looking at the stars, but whether or not I switch to those secondary tanks, either way, eventually, the oxygen will run out. And when it runs out, it runs out gradually. And when it runs out, I start to feel myself fading, my vision becomes hazy, and the one sun looks like two blurry suns. And I look at our space craft, and the space craft now looks like a tiny white speck, a small point of light, way far away, but a 'far away' that seems sort of close and easy to get to, except I'm too tired to try, and that feels good, because that's how the brain tells you to feel in moments like this, that's how—and I feel sleepy, and I feel slow, and I feel hazy, and I feel nice. And then my brain shuts off. And soon after, so do I. And then that's when I wake up.

No Way Around but Through
Scott Caan

Dramatic
Frank: Thirties

Frank is speaking to Rachel, who has asked him to tell her something that is honest about himself, that he really doesn't want to tell her.

FRANK: I've slept with way too many people. I sleep with everybody. Yes, it feels good, and yes, I've gotten very good at it, but so what. That's not the point. I also fall in love about once a month, and every time I tell myself this time it's going to be different. It never is, but I swear to God it feels like it is. Every time! So I started seeing the guy, not intimately . . . well, maybe intimately, but not like that. A doctor. A therapist. Who immediately took all the fun out of what I was doing and made me start to think that this was all very bad. And as much as I agree, I hate it and don't want to change. Because I have this very deep and very long catastrophic style of thinking that leads me to believe I'm just screwed. So I hate this guy and don't want to change. I think I've actually made that decision right this second. But at the same time I want different things, and I long for change and the actual process of mature adult coupling. So I'm either fucked, or something's going to change . . . The good news is, I truly believe that every time you do something stupid you're one step closer to never doing it again.

Information on this playwright may be found at www.smithandkraus.com. Click on the AUTHORS tab.

NORTH OF THE BOULEVARD
Bruce Graham

Seriocomic
Bear: Forties, African American

Bear, a security guard, is talking to his buddy Trip, who owns an auto shop. Bear did not vote for Obama.

BEAR: I feel sorry for Obama—I do. Those rich white men in Texas this is drivin' them crazy. Black man in their White House. Night Obama won the election one of 'em probably put an ad for snipers in *Soldier of Fortune.* Gonna' be riots and shit. This country'll be in serious disarray. Gonna' get ugly, Trip. Ugly-er. "A black President—ohhh . . . we're all gonna' hug and sing Kumbaya." Bullshit. You can feel the hate just percolatin' out there. Obama sneezes they're gonna' say he's startin' an epidemic. People be at each other's throats. You heard it here first. Hey, I'd like a black president. I just don't want one who looks like he's eight years old. Gimmie Morgan-fuckin'-Freeman, somebody like that. A little gravitas is all I'm askin'. Obama wants to be everybody's friend—fuck that. Another 9/11's 'round the corner and when it happens I want some rich old crazy white Republican mutherfucker in there. They try that shit again I want somebody in there gonna' go all Dr. Strangelove on their asses. You watch what happens when he opens up the borders. You think this neighborhood's got trouble now? Those people live across the street from you—right outta' the jungle. Never seen anybody that black. They're purple they're so black. Tellin' ya Trip, start sealin' up the borders.

Information on this playwright may be found at www.smithandkraus.com. Click on the AUTHORS tab.

NORTH OF THE BOULEVARD
Bruce Graham

Comic
Bear: Forties, African American

Bear, a security guard, is talking to his old buddy trip about a book he has found—The Tao of Pooh

BEAR: Fucked up nursery rhymes, right? When my kids were little—Kevin too, he watched 'em alla' time—Winnie the Pooh. Not till you're an adult you realize how fucked up the 100 Acre Wood was. Ya got that donkey—what's his name—Eyeore. He's a fuckin' manic depressive. Piglet's got the shakes. Owl's got Alzheimers. Christopher Robin—he's a little light in the loafers with those shorts and everything. Tigger, man, he's got like A.D.D. or somethin'. And Pooh's got a fuckin' eating disorder. I mean, kids think this is all so great—know what I'm sayin'—but that 100 Acre Wood was one fucked up place. But this book, see, it tries to put like a positive spin on it, know what I'm sayin'? See the Tao believes in harmony. Whatever life gives ya you try and find the positive in it. They call people the uncarved block. You take what you are—don't try and change it or anything—and then you have natural power. In other words, use what you got. I couldn't throw a football to save my life, but I could block, right. Who watched your blind side, huh Trip? You never got sacked from your blind side. Anyway, when I was onna' line there protectin' your ass, I found my "perfect order." I was in harmony with nature cause I was using my natural power. Like Pooh says in here, "A fish can't whistle and neither can I." There's nothin' wrong with that cause a fish ain't designed to whistle and if he tries all he's gonna' do is get frustrated and angry and fuck up everybody else's harmony.
   (tapping the book)

Some very serious shit in here. *(Pause)* So I'm tryin' to adjust my life here now, Trip, know what I'm sayin'? I mean, if I gotta' live in the 100 Acre Wood here I'm gonna' try and find what's positive. Quit wastin' my natural power with negative shit.

Information on this playwright may be found at www.smithandkraus.com. Click on the AUTHORS tab.

NORTH TO MAINE

Brenton Lengel

Dramatic
Kevin: Fifties

Kevin is hiking the Appalachian Trail with Adam, who has asked him if he carries a gun.

KEVIN: At some point, someone always tells a guy planning a thru-hike to bring a gun. I must've had at least twelve people tell me to bring a gun, including my brother. Guns are heavy. They're illegal in a lot of places, and you're really not going to use them for anything out here. Truth be told, I'm glad I don't have a piece . . . I think the worst part is how damaging they are to our spirit. Now, I don't mean none of that new-age "crunchy granola" shit. I mean the spirit of the hiker community. People back in "the real world" worry, because when they think wilderness, they think "no law," "no police," "total isolation," but that's just not true. If I slipped and broke my leg and couldn't go on, you can bet someone would be by to help me. It's not a question, it's a given. Hikers take care of hikers. But if we were all walking around here with our hands on our six-guns like it was the Wild Wild West, you can bet this place wouldn't feel the same. You put a gun in a man's hand, and there's always a part of his brain thinking about how and when he's going to use it. He's always waiting for that bear, or that psycho. He becomes afraid, introverted, and suspicious. It's just not worth having one. A gadget ain't gonna save your life. *You're* gonna save your life. Being safe out here isn't about having weapons. It's about being smart; it's about going with your gut. If I'm around someone I don't trust, I don't camp with them. If someone is giving me a bad vibe, I hike away. Simple as that.

Information on this playwright may be found
at www.smithandkraus.com. Click on the AUTHORS tab.

NORTH TO MAINE
Brenton Lengel

Dramatic
Nick: Twenty-seven

*Nick is hiking the Appalachian Trail with Adam, who is
seeking an adventure along the lines of the* Fellowship
of the Ring *but so far hasn't found it. Nick explains to
him that, in fact, he has.*

NICK: There are no wizards or orcs, but look: you are having
your adventure . . . do you believe in God? Well I don't,
and I figure we're better off without him. It's like what
Nietzsche said: in a universe without God, our lives have
no inherent meaning, other than what we impose. We are
the ones who make our lives great; WE take the chaos
around us and mold it into something beautiful. That's
what you're doing. You are on an adventure . . . that doesn't
change because there are no dragons or wizards. Hell, if
you ask me, you're better off without them. There's more
magic in these hills, or in Picasso, or Einstein, than in all
the fairies or gods ever imagined. You're an über-nerd,
but you're an über-nerd who's living life on his terms,
and I think that's pretty fucking cool. That drama with
your parents? It's fucked up, but you know what? It's
going to pass. Things are going to get easier. That's the
way life is. It's like climbing a goddamn mountain. You
haul your ass up the switchbacks until your clothes are
caked with salt, and your eyes are burning and blurry
from the sweat, and your legs are getting ready to mu-
tiny. You keep telling yourself that the summit is right
around the next corner . . . and it's not, but you'll get
there eventually. And no matter how bad it seems, and
how much your muscles scream for you to stop, you can
always take one more step. And when you get there, man
. . . you look out over the hills and the valleys and if it's
clear enough, it's like you can see forever; like you can

see through time. And the future and past are stretched out before you in all directions, and you say to yourself, "I climb mountains."

Information on this playwright may be found at www.smithandkraus.com. Click on the AUTHORS tab.

O<small>NE</small> N<small>IGHT</small>
Charles Fuller

Dramatic
Horace: Late twenties, African American

*Horace has been looking out for Alicia, a woman with whom
he served in Iraq who was raped there by three men, two of
whom she was able to identify, but the army dismissed her
charges against them. The two of them are homeless. The
shelter where they were staying burned down and they are
now in a seedy motel room. Here, Horace reveals why he
has been trying to save Alicia. He was the third man.*

HORACE: 'Started as a *joke,* that's all! You have to *come
down* from *killing people everyday*—break the monotony
of every hour—every minute!—You have to—to *fuck
something!*—Get it out of you! We wanted to—snatch
some of that *smart-mout*h from you and McCray! We
did all the killing, but you two got *commendations* for
driving up in a fucking gun-truck? That was our third
day under fire, and not one *'Grunt'* from 'A' platoon—
got anything but put down because of a *bitch Sergeant*
and her *bitch shotgun*! You shouldn't have been there in
the first place! *(pause, annoyed with himself)* I was in it
—and—but Frank and Terry said they wouldn't go unless
we went all the way—an' *I had to participate*! It was *my
joke*! Every day, *everywhere*—after all the bodies I left
rotting in the *'Sandbox'*- your face that one *night,* was all
I could see—I thought if I could find you, —I—I would
give you money—beg your forgiveness and *'walk off
down range'*, but you were homeless—helpless—and *So
beautiful*—I decided to stay for a minute—run interfer-
ence for you, lead the way, eliminate the *enemy*—like
I did in the *'SandBox'*. *(slight pause)* I hoped you'd
forget—I'm so sorry! I tried, Alicia *(pause)* I tried! I
kept the whole *world* off *you, Sarge*! *I* took down the
woman at the VA, when you needed somebody to speak

up for you! Who got the shelter at Ninety-three-thirteen? *I* made sure you could march through the mess of the application papers and your disability claims. *I* eliminated everything in your path—but the apartment was different, wasn't it? Where would *I* be once you got it? It was all for Louis! Who needs Horace then? Well, without me you're *nobody-nothing-nowhere*— understand?

Information on this playwright may be found at www.smithandkraus.com. Click on the AUTHORS tab.

POLLYWOG

John P. McEnemy

Dramatic
Gunther Jorbenadze: Twenty

Gunther, who teaches swimming at a Christian high school, tells how his family was massacred in the Republic of Georgia.

GUNTHER: We knew the separatists were coming so my mother hid me in closet on the top shelf. I was small and made myself smaller. Nekulai ran to get my father who I think was still in the quarry. I had never seen my mother so scared. She didn't want to go anywhere until my father was back. There was a UN cease fire so my father felt safe to leave us alone. And then the men came and they told her to take off all of her clothes and she started screaming. And I put my fists together in that dark shelf and I prayed to God. When I had my first communion—I remember kneeling on hard wood pew, talking to God in my head like he was some pal that could answer. "Thank you God for my parents, my new blue sneakers, and could you help make my dog feel better. Your friend, Gunther." And then in that closet while my mother wept in her own kitchen—I prayed again—more than I ever had before. "Please God, make these men go away. Don't let my mother cry. Don't let them hurt her. Don't let them do to me what they were doing to her." And then I heard my father and Nekulai run in and there was screaming and more pounding. I waited in the closet praying to God again. One last time: "Please make my family be alright. Please don't let me have to open the door, climb down, and see them dead. Please don't make me see my mother naked crying with shaking hands over my bleeding brother. Please don't make me see my father dead on the floor with his eyes still open. Please God." But God doesn't listen to my prayers. And if he did, he said: "I don't care, Gunther." So I know there's no God. At least there's no God that day. Not in Sukhumi.

Information on this playwright may be found at www.smithandkraus.com. Click on the AUTHORS tab.

ROMANCE IS DEAD
Daniel Guyton

Dramatic
Dr. Bainsbridge: Forties to Fifties

Dr. Edward Bainsbridge is a medical school examiner who has been caught fiddling with corpses. Here, he explains himself to a reporter.

DR. BAINSBRIDGE: Sex with dead people? You know, you . . . put it like that, it sounds awful. But, it's really not that bad. Of course, you . . . have to lubricate. But I think the biggest problem is the families. The families of the so-called dead. You'd think they'd let their loved ones rest in peace. Enjoy the afterlife for a while. But no! Instead, they've got to go . . . passing all these laws! "Keep your fingers off my Suzie." "Let my grandmother rest in peace!" And "Gerald! Oh Gerald! You've defiled Gerald!" *(pause)* Please. I knew that man when he was alive. If any man deserved defiling, it was him. He had a . . . stick up his ass the day he was born. Ironically, when I . . . made love to him, it was the least rigid he had ever been. He finally allowed himself, in my arms, to just relax. They say the dead have left their body, but that man was still inside it, let me tell you. And he loved every minute of it! *(pause)* I'm not a pervert. I simply have a predilection for experiment. And I've slept with other people too, you know. Mostly living. Of course, my ex-wife, she was . . . well, let's just say the corpses gave off more heat than she did! You can . . . put that in your magazine. Your newspaper. Whatever it is you call it. *(pause)* You know, I've read the things the papers say. You've been quite tasteful really. Quite . . . factual. I really can't complain. It was these other shits. Mike Gibson at the *Globe*. He wouldn't know the truth if it bit him on the ass! Lies and hearsay, that's all it is. Do you know the *New York Times* . . . *The New York Times*!

Claimed that I, quote, "allegedly had relations with half a dozen corpses, maybe more." End quote. *(Pause)* Half a dozen corpses. Where do I find the stamina? The . . . state of Arizona, on the other hand, has four counts of sexual misbehavior against me. Four. There's no six . . . seven . . . eight, or nine! So why don't you get your facts straight, *New York Times*? I thought you were paid to write the truth! *(pause)* Ah, but who bloody cares about the truth these days? It's all sensation.

SCOTT AND HEM IN THE GARDEN OF ALLAH
Mark St. Germain

Dramatic
Fitzgerald: Forty-one

F. Scott Fitzgerald is talking to Ernest Hemingway about his mad wife Zelda.

FITZGERALD: I never encouraged; I just didn't discourage. I'd write while she'd practice in her studio, playing "The March Of The Wooden Soldiers" over and over. It was a terrifying thing. She'd practice for ten, eleven hours a day, stared in the mirror like she hated her every move. She'd dance 'till her muscles spasmed. By then the only people she was talking to were Mary Stuart and William the Conqueror. I took a walk one morning and when I came back I found her on the floor, playing with a pile of sand. Picking it up, watching it slide through her fingers, not saying a word. She just looked up at me and smiled, the first time in forever. I brought her to the hospital and he Doctor told me, so matter of fact, "Your wife is mad". They tried every drug you can think of for starters. Then they injected horse blood into her spine. Hydrotherapy, insulin comas and electroshock, they kept trying no matter how much memory loss it cost her. If she had a few good days in a row I took her on trips. The last time we went to New York and stayed at the Plaza because it was familiar. She jumped into the Pulitzer Fountain. She said it called to her. The next morning I woke up to the Police pounding on the door. She was gone. So were all my pants. She told them I escaped an asylum and was holding her prisoner. Thank God they believed me. We found her in Central Park burying my clothes.

Information on this playwright may be found at
www.smithandkraus.com. Click on the AUTHORS tab.

SCOTT AND HEM IN THE GARDEN OF ALLAH
Mark St. Germain

Dramatic
Hemingway: Thirty-eight

Ernest Hemingway tells F. Scott Fitzgerald of his terror at not being able to write anymore.

HEMINGWAY: I shovel garbage every day and it stinks worse the more it piles up. A big case of depression. The "Writer's Reward." I think of what I did that was good, and I know I can't do it again. I think of the future and I don't see one. It's easy to look hard boiled in daylight but night's another thing. There are too many people in the dark. When I do sleep I'm a kid again, my Mother and Father tucking me in and I tell them I want to grow up to be anybody but them. Then I lay there 'till morning when I have a few drinks and stare at the paper again. You're right. That's the addiction. If I'm not writing I'm nothing. You know what my good Mother sent me on my birthday? My father's gun. Somebody must have cleaned it up, because if it were up to her she would have left his brains on the barrel. In the middle of the night sometimes I pick it up and put my finger on the trigger ready to pull it except it would make her too happy. Her misery's what I live for.

Information on this playwright may be found at
www.smithandkraus.com. Click on the AUTHORS tab.

Show Us Yer Tats
Kent Thompson

Seriocomic
Leon: Seventy

Leon Gabber, an old biker, explains his business methods to Janice, who pretends to be a health worker and claims to be Leon's long lost and unacknowledged daughter. Leon denies any knowledge of her.

LEON: What I do is sell information on gun control to anyone who wants to buy it. I'm like a pollster. What I do is dress up respectable . . . oh, yeah, I can do that. Even cut off my beard sometimes. You don't think I can wear a suit? I can. I was a school teacher once . . . you didn't find that out following me around? I'm surprised. I hated that fucking world. So I put on a suit and a tie and take a clipboard and go into the suburbs and knock at doors with my petition against gun control. The guy answers and I say I have this petition against gun control, does he want to sign it. Very often he says goddamn government of course he'll sign it. Sometimes I get a lecture, usually from a mingee-mouthed bitch who wants the world like her living room with nickknacks on glass shelves. But sometimes I meet this guy who's a gun collector, and he says, "shit, yeah, I'll sign your petition, goddamn government, wants to run our lives", and he's right about that, fucking cops, and then he says, "hey, you want to see my collection" and I say, "Yeah!" and he says "goddamn government is not getting my guns," and he invites me in to look at his Uzis and AK-47s, about which he knows what he thinks amounts to history. Russian assault rifles! Leningrad! "Geez," I say, "these are great." And he says, "you got to protect yourself. You got to protect yourself against the gangs come riding down the streets." With this, he says, "I can mow down a mob of Hell's Angels or Satan's Choice, you better believe it." And he signs my petition and tells me of other collectors who feel the same way he does, and I go to see them, too. You'd be surprised at the amount of firepower in any suburban neighborhood. Enough to repulse the assault on Leningrad or blow me all to hell when I come cruising down the street looking at his wife's tits while she's hanging up the laundry or his daughter's sweet brown legs while she's sitting in the porch lounger, bored out of her tree and getting squirmy at the sight of the Harley. He's got all this weaponry to keep his daughter up on her feet while I want her down on her back. Janice: You sell these insights into the suburban mind? Leon: I sell the fucking names and addresses of the guys who have the guns. I keep really careful records. And then, amazingly, maybe a year later, while he's at church or with the family out at the cottage, somebody breaks in . . . not me . . . and steals every last one of those AK-47s and every other bang-bang he has, and who gives a fuck if they're all fucking registered. The next thing you know that AK-47 is in the hands of some guy who rides a dirty Harley and is certifi-ably insane. *(pause)* Of course, I'm probably making up all this stuff just to make myself sound interesting. Call myself a kind of a gun-runner to girls with big tits. Gets them as excited as the Harley. They can hardly wait to spread their legs over a Harley.

Lawrence Harbison

SHOW US YER TATS
Kent Thompson

Seriocomic
Dog: Thirty-two

Recently fired undercover cop Bad Dog (Doug) is speaking to Leon. Dog has beaten up a man he caught robbing his apartment, and Dog's wife has left him, probably for another woman. The police department is squeezing Dog out of his pension.

DOG: So what happened was, I walked into my apartment, and the first thing I thought was: Jeeze! Somebody's here! And the first thought was *of course* Marcie. What the fuck is Marcie doing here, I thought to myself, and walked into the bedroom—and there the sonuvabitch was, going through my drawers. And the first thought was that he's looking for Marcie's panties because that's what guys do, eh? They break in and the first thing they steal are the underpants, then the stereo, the TV and stuff. But *of course* none of her stuff is there anymore, which *of course* pisses me off, and this guy is standing there with his face hanging out and a pair of my socks in each hand. He looks like a right idiot. Now, here's the funny thing. I level my gun at him and say, "freeze!" and he does, and then I go up to him and start hitting him with the gun barrel because I am so pissed off that he's got his dirty hand in Marcie's panties which aren't there anymore and in fact were someplace else when she was still around. Then I kick him in the shins because I am so pissed off and kick his Jesus feet right out from under him and he's down on the floor and I put the boots to him: Wham! Wham! Right in his nuts. Wham! I kick him in the face, I break his jaw, I kick him in the nose, break his nose. He's a total mess, and I wipe his blood off the toe of my boot on his shirt. And it's amazing— he never lets go of my socks. It really pissed me off and

99

he wouldn't let go of my socks. So I grab another pair of socks and shove them in his mouth and kick him out the door and down the stairs. It's all a matter of timing, you know? Say he'd robbed me before Marcie left and I'd caught him. I wouldn't have been so pissed off and he's just have been arrested and charged. He wouldn't have got the broken nose and broken jaw and miscellaneous lacerations. *(pause)* A man without a woman is mean, eh? He's still got my socks in his hands when he's out on the street and runs into a couple of uniforms who *of course* want to help him—he's such a bloody mess. He *of course* immediately confesses to stealing my fucking socks.

Information on this playwright may be found at www.smithandkraus.com. Click on the AUTHORS tab.

SILA

Chantal Bilodeau

Dramatic
Thomas: Forties, Canadian

*Thomas, a Coast Guard officer, has recommended his friend
Jean, a Canadian climate scientist now living in the U.S.,
for a lead position on an Environmental Assessment that
will evaluate the impact of oil extraction in the Canadian
Arctic. When Jean dismisses the opportunity, Thomas tries
to appeal to his patriotic sensibilities to win him over.*

THOMAS: The Danes are claiming Hans Island as their
own. The Russians have dropped a flag on the sea floor
of the North Pole. The U.S. is reviving an old dispute
over the offshore boundary line between Alaska and the
Yukon. And both the Americans and the Europeans refuse
to recognize Canada's sovereignty over the Northwest
Passage. Yeah, I think it's about territory. It's about na-
tional security, control, diplomatic relations and most of
all, money. Somebody's gonna drill, Jean. If it's not us,
it'll be the Americans, the Chinese, the Arabs, whoever
the fuck but somebody's gonna drill. There's too much
money at stake. If we wanna maintain sovereignty over
our Arctic territory, we need to establish a strong pres-
ence. Nunavut is huge. It has a very small population:
point zero one person per square kilometer to be exact.
There's practically no one around to say uh-uh, not here,
this is ours. Taking the lead in exploiting our resources is
one way to assert sovereignty. Having you, a Canadian
and one of our most prominent scientists, doing research
is another. It shows that we're interested. It shows that we
care. And as a bonus, it'll benefit the Inuit. You should
think about that.

A SNOWFALL IN BERLIN
Don Nigro

Dramatic
Coates: Forty-three, British

Coates is the screenwriter for an independent film. Formerly an up and coming playwright in Britain, he has come to America to make money writing films, and developed a desperate infatuation with Natasha, the brilliant Russian director, who is the only woman in the world he can't get to sleep with him. Here he is describing the career of one of his heroes, Fritz Lang, once a great director, finally a Hollywood hack. Coates identifies with Lang's sellout, and also possibly shares his murderous tendencies. Coates hates America and everything about it. He is smart, funny, charming, nasty, irresistible to most women, a cad, and very lonely and unhappy. He drinks. When he talks about Lang, he is really describing his own desperate failure.

COATES: It's true. I have fallen far beneath my station. You don't seem to appreciate what a significant figure I am, back in the civilized world, where at least thirty percent of the population can read the back of their cornflakes box. In Britain, I have been quite a celebrated playwright, which is to say, in order to make a living, I write movies. I am a serious artist, which in America means that I am patronized by cretins and plagiarized by vermin. The movies at home are stupid enough, I'll grant you, and abysmally dull, but nothing can match the obscenely expensive, relentlessly juvenile and borderline subhuman drivel they manufacture in this particular circle of Hell. Dying. I am dying, Egypt. My life is a charnel house. I scuttle like rats over piles of old bones. I came here for the money, and as soon as I got here, I realized what a terrible mistake I'd made, but every time I go to the airport, I have a panic attack. The world spins, and I have horrendous dreams of falling from a great height, like Kim Novak in *Vertigo,* or Satan, into the ocean. And then deep into the water. Into everlasting darkness. With those that God forgot. Natasha. Natasha is the answer. I couldn't resist her. Nobody can. Natasha is the ultimate challenge for a man like me. Incredibly sexy. Smoldering eyes. Clearly, fire inside. And yet touch her and she goes as rigid as a frozen squirrel. She will not let me in. Figuratively and literally. She drives me completely out of my mind. And she enjoys it. I won't say she does it deliberately, but she knows it's happening, and she takes a sort of dark pleasure in it. It's some manner of deeply twisted revenge, I think. Who knows? Women are always punishing some poor schmuck for something the last man did to them. But this one has turned it into art. For her, everything's a movie. She's a natural in front of the camera, too. She can cry on cue. Which leads one ask, are any of her emotions real? She could be so good at it that she even fools herself. What does it matter, if she gets what she wants? And she always gets what she wants. We need rain in this scene. Cue the rain. And it rains. She is the Queen of the Rainy Country. Don't be misled by her charms. She is very angry. Or very guilty. Or both. The most dangerous creature on the face of the earth is a woman who's been wounded. Utterly ruthless. So don't tell me to watch out, pal. You watch out. Don't say I didn't warn you. You stand warned.

A Snowfall in Berlin
Don Nigro

Dramatic
Coates: Forty-three, British

Coates is a screenwriter for the independent film the brilliant and beautiful Russian director Natasha is making. A serial seducer and predator upon vulnerable women, he is obsessed with Natasha, who refuses to sleep with him. He hates Americans, hates the movies, hates himself and pretty much everybody else. He is smart, funny, charming, smooth, and drinks too much. Here he is trying to warn Detective Mulligan who is investigating a murder on set, that Natasha is a very dangerous person. In fact, it might be Coates who is the dangerous person.

COATES: Fritz Lang, the great German director, with his eye patch and his stuffed monkey, footsteps echoing down a long corridor, enters the office of Josef Goebbels, Nazi Minister of Propaganda. Animal skins on the floor. Animal heads on the walls. Smell of expensive cologne. Out the window, the hands of a big clock. Goebbels greets him like an old friend, seats him in a leather chair, offers him a cigar, and apologizes for confiscating his movie, explaining that unfortunately he had a few problems with the ending. The Führer should come in at the end, defeat Dr. Mabuse and save the world. It's not enough that the villain goes insane. What does it prove that a person goes insane? Anybody can go insane. There is no moral lesson there. And I believe, Fritz, says Goebbels, that art must have a moral lesson. Art must uphold family values, good old fashioned conservative values. So if you could just make it a bit more uplifting, we might allow it to be released. And Fritz Lang says, as politely as he can, that he'd prefer not to. Goebbels smiles at him. I know, Fritz, that you are a good German at heart, he says. Those ugly rumors about your Jewish grandmother could not be true.

The Führer loved Metropolis, and Die Nibelungen so moved him that he sobbed in the arms of Himmler and said, at last, a man who will give us great Nazi films. So Fritz is drenched in sweat, thinking, Christ, he knows my grandmother was Jewish. I've got to get the hell out of here. If he'd just shut up I could run to the bank and escape to Paris. But this demented son of a bitch won't stop talking. And the hands of the big clock move slowly, slowly. But Fritz does manage to slip out of the country, and settles in Hollywood, where he discovers that if you play your cards right, you don't actually have to finish anything. Just bring in a new draft every six months and pretend to listen to some cigar chomping ignoramus puke out a bunch of rubbish and go home and do a couple of rewrites and bring it back and listen to the same moron criticizing the changes he told you to make, and you can stay on the payroll forever. You can live a very comfortable life if you just don't say no to these people. Just smile and nod and take their money. This is the only rule in Hollywood. Always take the money. Enjoy the orchestra playing while the ship is going down. So Fritz Lang spends the rest of his life beside his swimming pool, with his eye patch and his stuffed monkey, manufacturing garbage. The one thing that never changes is that, both in his previous life, as an artist, and his subsequent life, as a prostitute, the actors all hate him. The crew hates him. Sand bags keep dropping and just missing him. No matter where you go or what you do, the lunatic in your head comes with you.

Sousepaw

Jonathan A Goldberg

Dramatic
Waddell: Thirties

Rube Waddell, a former star pitcher in the major leagues, has wrecked his career with drink but is sober now and hoping for a comeback. He has enticed a carnival performer, Reptile Girl, to come to his seedy hotel room for a special performance of her act. Here, he tells her what made him decide to change his life.

WADDELL: I was down near Memphis when this storm hit. I was sleeping in Fire Station 11. Storm was tearing houses apart but then the dam burst and the waters came. We pulled some boats together but in a tangle of weeds was these little boys. I dove in and got to them. They grabbed on to me and nearly drown me. They was so scared they clawed onto my body as soon as I came close. I was handing them to the people in the boat—suddenly something pulled me under. Dragged to the mud and I looked down and I saw the drowned unsaveable angry dead pulling on. They asked why they had to die. Then they turned to snapping fish and turtles and snakes and gators. I realized how much of my life I wasn't using. How many of them would have had a better fuller life than me. How many of them could have built something or done anything but live as a drunk on the floor like a fire station dog. "But ain't I the best pitcher?" And they laughed a black burp at me that even underwater I could smell. And I decided to let them have me. To give into the mud. I gave up. Just as I let go a hand pulled me above the water. I guess I am a cork. They pulled me up my mouth greedy as ever for air. Like a new baby. And that's what I was. Then I went to fucking sleep and woke up a few days later. There's a secret for you.

Information on this playwright may be found at www.smithandkraus.com. Click on the AUTHORS tab.

SOUSEPAW
Jonathan A. Goldberg

Dramatic
Waddell: Thirties

Rube Waddell, a former star pitcher in the major leagues, has wrecked his career with drink but is sober now and hoping for a comeback. He has enticed a carnival performer, Reptile Girl, to come to his seedy hotel room for a special performance of her act. Here, he tells her that he's ready for his comeback.

WADDELL: To be good you need a challenge. You don't climb a mountain 'cause it's easy. No one got a medal from climbing the world's smallest mountain. The height makes the braver man. I can't be good pitching to a bunch of backwater boys. I need the real hitters. I need Ty Cobb and Billy Reigns. I need to feel the sweat of knowing that a wrong turn of the wrist and I'm lost. Challenge. They throw me gristle and think I'll smile like it's a prime cut. They think I'll choke it down and kiss their asses for the privilege. They give me this *chance.* A "last chance." A *good chance.* That's what he called it. *A good deal.* It ain't no deal. I wasted my own time, I understand that. I made peace that I should have been throwing the ball instead of riding a zebra around the zoo naked, fine. But now I'm ready. Ready to throw a ball like it's never been thrown.

Information on this playwright may be found at
www.smithandkraus.com. Click on the AUTHORS tab.

SOUTH BEACH BABYLON
Michael McKeever

Seriocomic
Simon: Forties

Simon, a choreographer/performance artist, addresses the audience before his latest piece is performed.

SIMON: I, um . . . I was all set to introduce this piece with a short but amusing anecdote about the fragility of an artists' ego. And then, I was going to thank Mr. Rosenfarb and his lovely wife . . . Lou. But, I'm not going to do any of that. Instead . . . I'm going to do this *(beat)* For the longest time, I've been asking myself, *why do we do it?* Why do we work so hard to produce something that brings in so little money . . . that so few people might actually see? And, the fact is, I know the answer . . . it's just every so often I lose sight of it. *(beat)* The writer Elizabeth Gilbert tells of how thousands of years ago—some think dating back to Ancient Babylon—performers would dance in these elaborately staged celebrations. There was no real reason for these events, no decided holiday or purpose for the performance, other than the simple joy of exploring one's art. A celebration of the artist's life, if you will. Now on rare occasions, during these celebrations, a performer would become so involved, so *enraptured*—so *in the moment* of the piece—that he would become transcendent. Artist and art would fuse together. Everything would just click. Body and soul and music would morph into one continual flow. It was almost as if something divine had taken over his body. And those people who were lucky enough to witness this would clap their hands together and shout, *"Allah, Allah." "God, God."* Because they understood that in these moments of rapture, when the artist was so connected with his craft, that they somehow transcended mere mortality and touched God. And God -

in which ever form you choose to define that word—was evident in their work. *(beat)* Over the years, the custom found its way to Northern Africa and then the Moors took it to southern Spain, where "Allah, Allah " somehow evolved into "Ole, Ole." *(beat)* Anyway, *that* is why we do it. That is why we continue to struggle to produce art, despite the most overwhelming of overwhelming obstacles. Because every so often—whether on stage or canvas or piece of paper—it happens. Artist and craft come together in perfect unison. One becomes the other. And in that remarkable moment: *Allah, Allah.* Or even *Ole, ole . . .* We touch God.

STARS AND BARMEN
Reina Hardy

Seriocomic
Rupert: Late twenties

Rupert, an astrophysics PhD student in a city where no one can see the stars, leaves his lonely post at a computer and explores the nightlife, gatecrashing parties and trying to get lucky. In this monologue, he strikes out with a succession of different women at different events.

RUPERT: Hey. Wow. HEY. Great party. I feel out-dressed by the crudités. I am Rupert, by the way. I'm an astrophysicist. I'm in the business of identifying large, bright and interesting objects. I had to inspect you more closely. I'm not saying you're large. You're very proportionate. And shiny. It's fascinating. So I take it you're involved in earthquake relief? Cool. Excellent. Inspiring. Listen, I'd really love to take your picture. It's for sort of a project. A comparative survey of women I'm attracted to at parties. Yes, that does sound slightly strange. I can be slightly strange, fair enough. Would you like a candy cigarette? They're totally legal. Ok. L'Chaim! To Rebecca on the day of her womanhood. I mean, Rachel. Thank you! She looks very mature. Not that I care about that. I'm here for the older cousins, and maybe even some of the cool aunts. I am very open to cool aunts. They have all kinds of auntly experience . . .
   (He stares at something large and unusual.)
What *is* that? I mean, it's a 20-foot Pentakis dodecahedron made out of tinfoil, but what's it doing at a party? Is it trying to say "Listen, this party is way beyond you. You do not understand this party. You could be having a transcendent experience here if you weren't a total and complete imposter." Not that you look like an imposter, you look very appropriate. Appropriate, yet approach-

able. You have one of those faces. You know, one of those faces where probably crazy people just start conversations with you on the bus out of nowhere? Yeah. Well, it's been nice talking to you.

Stars and Barmen
Reiny Hardy

Seriocomic
Rupert: Late twenties

Rupert, an astrophysics PhD student, is up all night trying to get lucky, playing hooky from work to crash parties and look for girls. But at this party, he's found a girl that he wants to avoid: Elaine, a weird, prickly and confrontational woman, who, in the last scene, came into his office and demanded that he pay her for sex. In this monologue, Rupert hides from Elaine in the bathroom.

RUPERT: How big is the universe? How fucking big is the universe, is my question? In the bad old days of the nineteen nineties, some people thought that the universe might be finite but unbounded, a big sheet of space time curved around a gargantuan but theoretical beach ball, and that if you stood still enough, for long enough, and had a good enough telescope, you could see all the way around the beach ball to the back of your own head, and then you could jizz in your pants because you officially Knew it All. But in the heroic age of the early 2000s, we had a long hard look at the sky, and as it turns out, we know jack about it all, or at least, the size of it all. We know that it's expanding at 71 kilometers per second per megaparsec. We know that we can see about about 93 billion light years of it. But as for how big it is, we only know that it's bigger than that. So my question is, given that the universe is either infinite, or really, really unfathomably big, how is that out of all the women in the universe that I could meet, at all the parties in the universe that I could crash, I would run into the one woman I know who is a dangerous fucking nut job?

STELLA AND LOU
Bruce Graham

Dramatic
Donnie: Thirties

Donnie is at a funeral home. O'Reilly, one of the regulars at Lou's Bar, has died and Donnie, who is getting married, tells Lou and the paltry group of other "mourners" what he thinks of O'Reilly and his miserable life.

DONNIE: I'm sorry, Lou, but he was. Bonafide . . . mint condition asshole. He was a miserable old bastard. Never cared about anybody but himself. I don't know why ya put up with him, Lou? Should'a made him go down the Shamrock. He'd of fit in great there.
(Thinks a moment.)
How could ya ever walk out on your family—never send a couple bucks. End up sittin' in bar every night 'cause ya got nothin' else. And you guys didn't see his apartment. I wanted to take a bath when I got home. Lou, am I lyin? I mean, look around. Guy his age should have forty, fifty people here at least. Nine guys. Barely enough ta carry the box. Nine guys—that's his whole life right here. And we're not even . . . friends. We just drank with the guy. By tomorrow nobody's gonna' know Reilly even existed. Nobody's gonna' miss 'em. Just a . . . miserable . . . lonely old man . . . sittin' in a bar. I told you I wasn't good at this, Lou.
(Looking out at the guys)
Okay, lemmie get somethin' off my chest here. Ever since I told you guys I was gettin' married you been givin' me a hard time. Walt, Shooter - everybody but Lou—bustin' on me. "Whatta' ya wanta' get married for?" Fact that you're all married's got nothin' to do with it, right? But you're all, "World's fulla' chicks. Don't be stupid. Stay a bachelor.

STUPID FUCKING BIRD

Aaron Posner

Dramatic
Con: Early twenties

Stupid Fucking Bird is a contemporary version of Chekhov's The Seagull. Con is the Konstantin Treplev character. He has been asked why he wants to change the world.

CON: Are you kidding me? Are you kidding me? Why do I want to change the world? Is that what you are actually asking me? Have you seen the world lately? I mean actually, actually seen it? Stupidity. Greed. Corporate dominance. Selfishness and neediness achieving new heights never before even imagined. Old forms. Old forms of everything, always being called new, but never actually *being* new. And new technologies and media onslaughts and and and *breakfast cereals* appealing with assassin-like accuracy to every worst impulse human beings have been subterraneanly cultivating for the past ten thousand years. *(Pause)* Why do I want to change the world? *(Pause)* BECAUSE IT NEEDS CHANGING! And once upon a time, somewhere, maybe in Eastern Europe—at least in the Eastern Europe of my imagination—"The Theatre" was something that Could maybe be some tiny, tiny, tiny part of that . . . and it has got to find its way to be that again or it should go the way of the dodo and the bell bottom and the newspaper and just GO AWAY!

Information on this playwright may be found
at www.smithandkraus.com. Click on the AUTHORS tab.

SUNSET BABY

Dominique Morisseau

Dramatic
Kenyatta: Fifties, African American

Once a famous radical political activist, Kenyatta has recently finished a long stretch in prison, during which his daughter Nina grew up without him and his wife Ashanti X, a political activist as famous as he, descended into drug addiction which led to her death. Kenyatta wants two things. He wants to reconnect with his daughter and he wants the un-mailed letters he thinks Ashanti may have written to him which, since her death, may be quite valuable. He is making a series of video recordings explaining his life to Nina. This is one of them.

KENYATTA: I always believed revolution was possible. I dreamed about it. Since childhood. Since I saw brother Kwame Ture speak at the community center by my block. He was no longer Stokley Carmichael by then. Dashiki and bearded. Skinny but a massive man to me. Long and brown and a face that looked like it carried its own light. He was the beginning. His voice was my awakening. Asked me to defy my complacency and take a role in the system. I was just a knucklehead kid then. Stealing snacks from the corner store and trying to bag girls for bragging rights. But that day . . . brother Kwame . . . I swear he saw through me. His eyes undressed my soul. His words grabbed me by the throat. He demanded me to question my behavior and the conditions of my people. He said, in that liquid voice of his, "No man can give another man his freedom." Freedom would be something we had to determine, and take, for ourselves. Freedom for me and my people. All of our people. ll power to all the people. And power is a cycle that needs to be rotated. Re-distributed. It would not happen in my lifetime, I thought. This freedom that I demanded . . . Whatever it was supposed to be, I might not ever touch it. But there was a plan. Plant my seed into a warrior woman who was as powerful as the sun. Build the revolution in the offspring. Because life is not a line. It is a circle. A cycle. And you are the next phase. The untainted, un-wilted next phase. You are the change. Do you hear me? You are my change. You are everything.

Information on this playwright may be found at www.smithandkraus.com. Click on the AUTHORS tab.

SUNSET BABY

Dominique Morisseau

Dramatic
Damon: Early thirties, African American

Damon, a drug dealer and hustler is talking to Nina, his girlfriend and partner in crime, who is the daughter of two famous radicals. Her mother is dead and her father, who just got out of prison, wants her letters. These may be quite valuable. Nina won't give them to him. Damon wants her to hit him up for money for them, so they can escape the life they've been leading. DJ is Damon's son, who lives with his mother.

DAMON: DJ is safe with me, Nina. I make sure he's taken care of. Got people lookin' out for him. That's the best I can do, right now. And you safe with me, too. You are, Nina. I know you think I be tryin' to gas you, but that ain't it. I'm too old to be tryin' to play you. I'm too old for all of this. These streets ain't for neither one of us no more. I swear to God—if I see another pair of shoes over some telephone wires I'ma lose my fuckin' mind. Kids do that shit to be stupid now. Don't even have no significance no more. Never know what it means now. Used to know—that's a hot block. Used to know somebody got robbed for they sneaks. Now you never know. These kids play by some stupid rules. Codes and honor don't mean shit to them. Whose set is whose—don't matter. They runnin' 'round like a bunch of pawns on a chessboard and don't even know the shit ain't real. Don't even know it's all a game. Shootin' each other over whatever . . . not abiding by nobody's laws . . . 5-0 or the streets. They just reckless . . . and they're the new leaders of the corner game. To hell with that. They can have this shit cuz I can't do it, Nina. And I'm not gonna do it. I don't want this no more. I want you. That's it. You and me . . . . and enough to know my son's alright. That's it. Nina, listen to me here. I'm tellin' you straight up. You can't hold onto this grudge for the rest of your life. Ashanti ain't live free, Nina. Ain't that what she always used to say? She don't know what free is . . . never did. But maybe . . . maybe she know it now. And you can let her go. Give them shits up. Give 'em to the man they was intended for. Maybe that's the peace she get. Nina, why's this gotta be hard? Why's you and me gotta be hard? It's simple. Let them pay you back. They took from you—a whole lotta years of trouble on your mind. A whole lotta nights of stress—for what? Cuz you had to hustle, that's what. Pay your way on your own and figure out how to survive. And that's you, baby. That's not them. You still here and alive and survivin' cuz of you. Cuz you a bad bitch. And when you runnin' off with me—it's nothin' we can't have. I'ma take care of you. Give you the life you been dreamin' of.

Information on this playwright may be found at www.smithandkraus.com. Click on the AUTHORS tab.

Sᴜɴsᴇᴛ Bᴀʙʏ

Dominique Morisseau

Dramatic
Damon: Early thirties

Damon is a petty thief and drug dealer. He is upset that he missed his son's birthday and wants reassurance from his girlfriend and partner in crime, Nina, that he isn't the lowlife scum his son's mother called him.

DAMON: He turned eight today. Eight years old. Eight years since I helped the doctor cut his cord. Eight birthdays and eight Chucky Cheese parties and eight candles on a fuckin' cake. Seven times I remembered. The eighth one . . . . I fuckin' forgot. I could say Rene set me up with that one but fuck it. Does it matter? I could say she usually calls to tell me the plan . . . usually asks me to buy the cake or book the arcade or foot the bill. This time she let me bake. Planned everything behind my back. Didn't ask me for shit. Knew I'd forget. Had too much on my mind this time. She was countin' on that. Knew I was plannin' to move away with you. Started arguing with me again. Been broke up over two years and she still on that jealous shit. Wouldn't let me speak to DJ no time this whole week. Every day I call, she got it so he's too busy. "In the bath" "Doin' his homework" "Visiting his cousins" "Asleep in the bed." I let the shit roll off. Know we working these last few deals. Figure I can focus and then holler at my son when I'm outta this shit for good. See him with a clean conscious for once. And what the fuck I do? I forget his eighth birthday. Day he ain't never gettin' back. Not neither one of us. And I showed up to his party late. Shit was over. No present. No nothin'. And still he came and hugged me. Like I was the gift. I was the muhfuckin' gift. *(pause)* I ain't never felt so unworthy. But that's my mans, right? Devoted son regardless of my bullshit. *(pause)* I wonder when he playin' this shit back later in life, will he remember I was late. Will he remember I forgot and showed up empty-handed? Or will he just remember I was there. Rene said I ain't shit. Ain't shit but a low life muthafucka. Ain't worth a damn as a man or a daddy. She probably tellin' that shit to DJ too. *(beat)* I wonder how long til' he believe it . . . *(beat)* You think I ain't shit Nina?

Information on this playwright may be found at www.smithandkraus.com. Click on the AUTHORS tab.

The Boat in the Tiger Suit
Hank Willenbrink

Dramatic
Herman: Late forties to fifties

It is Herman's funeral and his family has gathered together to try to mourn their absentee father. Just before this monologue, the family has opened Herman's closed casket to find nothing inside. Herman's ghost appears from a door in the floor and tells how he died and why no body was found. He is speaking to the audience.

HERMAN: First day in the army you know what they teach you? How to be a part of the team. Know why? The scariest thing out here is isolation. You go too far, you get the supply line cut off, they cut off your head. They don't teach you the way that you're taught in school. They shave your head. They make you the same as everyone else. You look at yourself and say—look at you, asshole. You're no different. Later on they yell that at you. They know how to get the point across. You run until you puke and then you run some more. It's a good thing they shaved your head because it's hotter than Texas. I ran next to a woman from Russia who had moved to Texas when she was a baby. She says that Texas is hotter than two rats fucking. Later she told me the phrase "hotter than two rats fucking" was her favorite English phrase. After that she said that my ass looked hotter than two rats fucking. I told her that I wasn't into women anymore. She asked why. I said I was married. The first time they sent me over, everything was already over. It was like going to a party at someone else's house and no one is there and you've gotta clean everything up and you don't know where the serving trays go. They didn't tell us where we were going. Just loaded everyone up into humvees with blindfolds on more to protect our eyes than anything else and dropped our asses off in the middle of this jungle. I swear I had

121

sand in every orifice imaginable but by the time I pulled off the mask, you couldn't see anything but green. The kind of green that lawns look in magazines. The kind that the jungle looks in picture books and nature programs. And it was about that time that I realized that this wasn't a picture book or a tv show or a magazine that we were actually in a jungle and that the jungle had materialized out of the desert like, well, like someone turning water into wine. And it was beautiful. A big marble fountain in the middle was the only thing that looked like it had been touched by man tho I assume that the whole thing must've been man-made because how the hell else does a jungle get out in the middle of a land that God forgot? There were three of us. The specialist, Natasha, and my buddy Eugenio. Natasha had a bunch of sunblock on because like my family she burned easily. Any insect that came within ten feet stuck to her so that she turned into a human flystrip. So she was swatting and bitching and Eugenio and I are laughing at her. The orders are to secure the area and since nothing is going on, we decide it's secure. Eugenio lays down his pack. Natasha finally stops swatting and suddenly a sense of calm seems to fall, and after a while they're both dozing like children in the sun; like kids do after a long day at the lake when the sun has finally been enough and there's been so much fun had that there's no choice but to shut your eyes, because really what else in the world could compare; I decide that I've gotta taste the water coming out of that fountain. The way the sun catches it, you can see right through it like it was made outta glass. So I take my canteen, dip it into the water, and once it's good and full, I put it to my lips and I swear to you I have never tasted anything so sweet in my life. Time seems to stop and I can feel that water moving down my throat, I swear to God, I can feel the water going into each of my little cells and making it wet, making it breathe, making it turn alive again. And then I hear it: from under the brush, a low, guttural growl. Maybe it was me that heard it. Then: 18

there it is again. I look over and I'll be damned if there isn't a motherfucking tiger poking his monstrous head out from under the green canopy. It's then, right then, that I get the feeling that I've never had before and that I'll never have again: that we truly are not safe here. That we are just visiting and that no matter what we do, we will never be back.

Information on this playwright may be found
at www.smithandkraus.com. Click on the AUTHORS tab.

THE BOAT IN THE TIGER SUIT
Hank Willenbrink

Dramatic
Gene: Thirties to early Forties

At the funeral of Herman, Gene's fellow solider and inamorata, the family has opened the casket to discover there is no body inside. Prior to this speech, Gene has had a confrontation with Dave which has leads to a physical struggle during which a finger has fallen out of Gene's pocket. In this speech, Gene tells of Herman's death and why there was no body in the casket.

GENE: When you're all garbled up. When they can't tell who you are. When a tiger eats you and there's nothing left. You'd be surprised how much we look the same. But, then again, maybe you wouldn't. When you're like that, just parts of a body. So maybe it's just as well that force you to forget who you are in the army. That you forget who you are, because you become the role you play. Some are the brains, some are the golden ones, some are the duds. You are what you do. Fact of the matter is that you're a family in as much as you don't care to be anything else. Being anything else is just that anything else which might as well be nothing which is what it is. So youdo what you do. And what does it matter what the truth is, or when anything happened? It's all the same. Same same. You think it's time passing, but it's just you falling apart. I knew that this was him, because he was married, so there was a wedding ring at some point right here. Right on his knuckle. Which is all that's left. And that's ironic, because the reason he signed up was to get away from who he was and the reason we know who he is, is because of what he tried to get away from. I told them I wanted to return. To explain to the family what had happened. They let me go, but said it was confidential.

What was confidential, I asked. We can't let the American People know that tigers are eating people over here, they said. But it's his family, I replied. And he was one of ours, they told me. It's true, I said. He was ours.

Information on this playwright may be found at www.smithandkraus.com. Click on the AUTHORS tab.

The Boat in the Tiger Suit
Hank Willenbrink

Dramatic
Herman: Late forties to fifties

Years after Herman's death, his son Rene has entered into a relationship with Herman's former inamorata, Gene. While Gene and Rene appear to have a very comfortable existence, Gene and Herman's relationship remains a secret to most of Rene and Gene's friends. In this speech, Herman appears as a ghost to warn his son that Gene is slipping away.

HERMAN: We didn't fuck. It wasn't like that. That, you know, carnal. I'm not saying that I wouldn't have done it. I probably would have. Would have had to get some guidance. It's weird to talk to your son about sex. And then about the same person that you . . . how do you love a man? Is it so much different than loving a woman? It didn't feel too different, but what do I know? It's important to know how things start to know how they'll end. You need to try to remember the beginnings of things and if I could remember the beginning of things, then you might have a chance, a shot, at understanding what the end of things are too. Like is the minute that you fall inlove so much different from the moment that your life falls apart. From experience? No. It's not. All this talking about letting things go and look who's listening to the old man ramble, ramble ramble. You know your Mom went to see Gene. Just a couple minutes ago. I looked over and shewasn't there. Yeah, that's right we live together in the afterlife. I can'ttell if its heaven or hell, but honestly it doesn't really matter. I don't know what they talked about, but figured yo should know in case your world becomes something that you don't like in the morning. And if that happens. I recommend you forget about letting the past go and do what your old man says to do: run.

Information on this playwright may be found
at www.smithandkraus.com. Click on the AUTHORS tab.

THE BOXER

Merridith Allen

Dramatic
Tyrone: Early thirties

Tyrone is the heavyweight boxing champion of the world. This is an interior monologue as he is fighting a challenger named Horatio.

TYRONE: Get up, Horatio! We about to tango now. This time I lead! Hold tight, Horatio. You got it comin.' Hold tight, hearin' the judges at their table, lights flashin' on our fists collidin' on the dance floor. Hold tight, cause I know where you open now, son. Gut check. *Pop!* Got you now, up against the ropes. Hold tight, but not to me— huggin' ain't for brothers fightin' to the end, man. Ref breakin' us up knows what's about to go down. Listen to that crowd—all on their feet now. My wife right down in front, watchin' her man in the white trunks. You got a woman here, Horatio? Where she at? Look into her eyes—say you're sorry without words. She ain't got a hero up on this stage, oh no sir, she ain't got no God. Cause I see you movin. I know the shuffle of your feet. Me and my man, we gotchu now. I let you slide out from under me. There you are, center ring. Ready, boy? Cause here I come. Floatin' like Mohammed Ali. You go—one, two, one, two, punch, my hands up high to block. Thought you blinded me good, didn't you? Think I'm coverin' cause I ain't got no vision left. Wanna see how wrong you are, Horatio? Go ahead, I know what you waitin' for. Lower my right hand a little, open shot, right? That's what you want. Well here you go. Shuffle up, jab, shuffle, jab, lean right, about to fake a fist comin' up. I let you, boy. Move my eyes right too. Think I don't know what's comin'? So there goes your shoulder and I come in, shuffle left, jab, jab, punch, jab, punch, jab, uppercut—now you back on the ropes. Look at me smile, Horatio. Look through that blood in your eyes. Here it come now. You watchin? Where it gonna come from? Right? Left? Move those eyes side to side—Ref ain't pullin' me away this time. Look out from below, my friend. Look out from Hell. That's the last you see before the lights get you. Before you goin' down, slidin' all over the ropes. You don't see me step back, do a little dance cause I know you ain't gettin' up. I took your tricks, fool. I took your tools. Whatchu got left now? Think those buckets up the mountains gonna save you from a real champ? No chance! You done, boy. You done.

Information on this playwright may be found at www.smithandkraus.com. Click on the AUTHORS tab.

THE CALL
Tanya Barfield

Dramatic
Peter: Forties

Peter and his wife are hosting a dinner party for another couple. He has recently been to Africa, and he tells his guests of a terrible thing that happened while he was there.

PETER: We were supposed to be volunteering, that didn't last long. Helping farmers irrigate their land. We're there a month and the organization asked us to contribute our *own* money to volunteer which we didn't have; well, we *did*, but—anyway, there were all these inner-politics so we quit, we travelled. We didn't go on safari if that's what you're asking. One time, I remember, out of nowhere, we got invited to this family's house for dinner. David made friends with *everyone*—and somehow through hand-signals, we get invited. But then, we don't go. But, we're both sick, heatstroke and we're chugging Pepto Bismol, so we don't go. A couple of days later, we go. The directions are: "Such and such village. The house near Kafele's house" but nobody knows who Kafele is. We wander around calling out, "Kafele? Kafele?" Seems like Kafele isn't actually important; he's just some guy. Eventually, we get there, apologize for not coming when we were supposed to; the wife's crying. Her eyes are puffy and the husband looks like he's been crying, too. And their daughter is so frail, she looks like she hasn't eaten in weeks. It turns out—now these people are *very* poor, they have *nothing,* their farm is barren—it turns out they slaughtered their last goat for our dinner. And we didn't show up. It was a*wful.* But they forgive us; they're so nice we feel like they're our long lost family but nobody really says anything because we don't speak the same language; we just use hand signals. We stay until it's late, then we leave their straw hut, go back to our hotel room, slip into our cozy beds and go to sleep. After a month—no, actually more, we're still talking about it, so we decide to buy them a goat. We try to push the goat up the hill but we fail. Goats are very stubborn. So we hire a goat herder. We finally get there, they are so appreciative, they start to cry. And . . . their daughter is missing, and . . . we ask where she is. She died.

THE CURIOUS CASE OF THE WATSON INTELLIGENCE
Madeleine George

Dramatic
Merrick: Fifties

Merrick, something of a crank, is explaining why he is running for office.

MERRICK: I mean look, we've *all* been lulled into a false sense of security, me included. I know how it is. You can go for years not really getting it, feeling like, I'm fine, I'm in this, sure, but I'm in it for a reason. Yeah I gave up a little bit of my liberty, yeah I maybe gave up a little bit of my autonomy, not to say my manhood, for the sake of this relationship, but it's good for me in the long run why? Because they have my best interests at heart. They're looking *after* me. They have smart notions of what will be a good use of my money, and really what do I know, I'm just an innocent little taxpayer who only has the experience of my own private life, how would I know what it might mean to put together something big and complicated like a *government*. Let them worry about appropriations, after they've slipped their clammy hand into my pants pocket every fifteenth of April and thieved forty percent of my annual dignity, annual *salary* I mean but that's a funny slip. And then one day you wake up and boom, the "government," that repository of your trust and fidelity and hard-earned fucking cash pardon my French, is collapsing, is imploding before your very eyes. Deficits. Austerity measures. Cutbacks and shutdowns. Turns out they *didn't* so much know what they were doing. Turns out their notion of what to do with your money was no more sophisticated than yours would have been, except that it included deception and corruption and shameless waste and mismanagement on a scale you never could have dreamed up on your own. Where's your money now? Gone. Where's your trust? Gone. Eaten away gradually at first, suspicion by suspicion, and finally gutted, throat to nuts, by a single sudden act of betrayal. *(pause)* I'm talking about the bailout of Wall Street. And now you're asking yourself, if you have half a brain, why should these institutions even exist? They said they were here to serve me but they're not serving me, they're screwing me, so why do I keep funding them? Why do I keep paying taxes to maintain them when all I want to do is dismantle them? So *that's* why I'm running. To dismantle the institutions that have enslaved us and humiliated us and conned us out of our money for far too long.

THE GOD GAME

Suzanne Bradbeer

Dramatic
Tom: Forties

Tom's old college chum, Matt, works for the Republican nominee for President. Matt wants Tom, a U.S. Senator, to agree to be the Vice Presidential running mate, even though Tom is considerably more liberal then the nominee. The candidate, a conservative, can accept a running mate with differing views than his—but only if Tom is willing to trumpet his sincere Christianity on the campaign trail. Tom does not have much use for this idea, as he thinks it will be phony. His wife Lisa is present.

TOM: Thomas Jefferson did not believe that Jesus was divine, either. Jefferson did not believe that Jesus Christ was the son of God. But this did not keep him from quoting Jesus. Or from quoting the Bible. Actually, here's an interesting fact—Jefferson made his own Bible. He did. He literally, with a razor, cut and pasted his own Bible. He left out all the miracles: no virgin birth, no resurrection: he cut out all that abracadabra and hocus-pocus—
    (to Lisa)
His words, Lisa, his words—and he made a Bible of what Jesus actually said. And what Jesus actually said—and did—was pretty damn great. So let's be clear: I am not debunking Jefferson, I obviously agree with Jefferson. But give me credit for a little judgment, Matt: this is my home, and I hope that I can say what I like, in my own home. And this is my wife, Lisa, whom I believe you know. And there is no one—no one—I respect more, but because of that, there is also no one that I can be as unfiltered with. We enjoy sparring—sometimes we enjoy it more than other times—but she helps me see the world with different eyes, and I hope that I do the same for her. And because you're here, and on such an

occasion, you get the benefit of things that I would not say outside of these walls. Not because I'm ashamed of them, but because they're *private*. It is not my neighbors' business what I believe. In fact, it was Jefferson who said it best, "It does me no injury if my neighbor says there are 20 gods—or—no god. It neither picks my pocket nor breaks my leg."

Information on this playwright may be found at www.smithandkraus.com. Click on the AUTHORS tab.

The Hunter's Moon
Frederick Stroppel

Comic
Shep: Early thirties

*Shep is a hapless loser type who's hanging out in a neigh-
borhood bar late at night. It's close to Halloween, and when
Shep gets scared by his friend Cooney wearing a werewolf
mask, it prompts him to relate a story to Cooney and the
bartender Jimmy about his frightening encounter with what
he believes was a real wolf some years earlier.*

SHEP: I had a very bad experience with a wolf. I was up in the
Catskills. It was one of those "Re-Live Woodstock" festivals. Except the bands sucked. Anyway, I was in this tent,
with this fat chick, and she was snoring like a bull. I couldn't
get to sleep, but it was her tent so I couldn't make an issue
of it. So it's the middle of the night, and I hear something
sniffing around outside, and I try to ignore it, I'm thinking
it's just a raccoon or something, but then I hear this water
trickling, and I realize it's pissing right on the tent! And I
guess she didn't set it up right because it's leaking right
through. So I jump out, ready to chase the little bastard off,
and right there in front of me is the biggest fucking wolf I
ever saw. We're like eye to eye. And it starts showing its
teeth. And I'm like, "This is it. I'm dead." Plus I'm totally
naked, so he's got, you know, the whole smorgasborg to
pick from. Anyway, the fat chick—her name was Patsy,
as I recall—she leaps out of the tent with this crossbow—I
don't know where the fuck she got that—and she screams,
"yaaagh!" and fires an arrow, totally misses the wolf—I
think she hit somebody's car—but the wolf gets spooked
and runs off. So I survived. But that was it for me with all
the outdoor festivals and Being-One-with-Nature shit. You
know, give me suburbia or give me death.

Information on this playwright may be found
at www.smithandkraus.com. Click on the AUTHORS tab.

THE HUNTER'S MOON

Frederick Stroppel

Dramatic
Man: Mid-forties

The Man has entered a bar late at night looking for his brother. A mysterious, somewhat sinister figure who claims to be a cop, he starts up a conversation with Katie, the only girl in the bar; there's a full moon outside, and it leads the Man to recall a girlfriend he once had, and what happened to her during a full moon.

MAN: I had this girlfriend, Catherine. I was about 28 at the time, so she must have been 24, 25 . . . Beautiful girl. Hair a lot like yours. But spacey. Especially around the full moon. I was a cop on the beat then, and she didn't like my hours, I was never around, pulling double-shifts, she was worried about me . . . the usual bullshit. And I said what I always said, every girlfriend I ever had: "If you can't deal with it, don't." So she didn't. After a while I missed her, I wanted her back—she was the one, you know? But she wasn't interested. She was seeing someone else, this piece of shit character, he was a broker or something, lots of money. I said fine, if that's what you want. So one night, the story goes, they went out to Jones Beach to go swimming. Skinny-dipping. Full moon, like I said. But the funny thing was, it was cloudy, so you really couldn't see the moon. So nobody really knows what happened—she was in the water, and she got a cramp, and there were these rip tides coming through, and he couldn't see her. He might have been drunk or coked-up, no one's really sure—he was fucking useless under the best circumstances, anyway, and . . . she got swept away, and that was it. Drowned. They found her body all the way out in Rockaway. She should have stayed with me. She'd be happy now. She'd be alive.

Information on this playwright may be found at www.smithandkraus.com. Click on the AUTHORS tab.

THE NORTH POOL
Rajiv Joseph

Dramatic
Dr. Danielson: Forties

Danielson is Vice-Principal of a large public high school, speaking to a student, a transfer student from the Middle East, Khadim, who has been asked to say after school in his office for a detention. Danielson has removed a map from his office wall to reveal an old mysterious metal door. Khadim has asked him if it's possible to enter the door.

DANIELSON: Once upon a time, there were crawl spaces connecting every major room in this giant school. Now, the doors are sealed shut. But the tunnels are still in there, like the arteries or veins of this place, leading down into the basement and then deeper down underground . . . to the North Pool. Ever hear of the North Pool, Khadim? Well, it *isn't* a pool. It's a bomb shelter. Back in the 50's . . . people were scared of . . . you know . . . annihilation. Why do you think they called it a pool if it wasn't a pool? It sounds better. *Let's go to the BOMB SHELTER* would freak kids out. There would be drills. Kids would crawl through these tunnels, scurrying down into the bowels of Sheff High. Where they'd all gather in this giant bathtub of concrete that would supposedly keep them safe from nuclear holocaust. Crazy times those were, huh? I think it's a piece of history. Cold War History. A relic of the past. But also, for me . . . . It's a reminder. Fundamentally the walls of this school should protect its students. I believe that. If it's the end of the world out there . . . then the deepest part of this school—the heart of Sheff High—should be a place where you can go to be safe.

Information on this playwright may be found
at www.smithandkraus.com. Click on the AUTHORS tab.

The North Pool

Rajiv Joseph

Dramatic
Khadim: Late teens

Khadeem is of Middle Eastern descent, but educated all over the world. He has been held after school for a detention in the office of Dr. Danielson, a white, middle aged Vice Principal, who hasn't seen much of the world. Danielson has been badgering Khadim, trying to figure out why the young man abruptly dropped out of an exclusive prep school and began coming to this large public high school.

KHADIM: I met this guy, this merchant, he was moving to Guinea. He sold a lot of things, and one of the things he sold was parrots. These little green parrots are all over the place in Guinea. Over there, you can buy them for like 2 dollars. In America, they cost like 400 bucks apiece. So we set up this thing, me and him. I got back to the States, and I went to this pet store and asked the owner if he wanted to buy those birds for 300 bucks. And then I had my guy in Guinea ship me the birds. You can't do that without proper licensing, so what he did was, he took 20 birds and this PVC piping. And he poked little breathing holes in the them. And then shoved the birds into the piping. He fit 20 birds in three lengths of it. He packaged it and mailed it to me. Except I had him mail it to Eagleton, because if my parents saw it, they'd open it. Most of the birds would die, but say you get one or two that make the voyage . . . I'd make some money. Once, though, a package got lost in the mail for awhile and then showed up at Eagleton and it stunk. And so the headmaster opened it and shook the PVC and ended up with 20 dead birds all over the place, most of them with maggots all in them. It was nasty. That's why I left Eagleton. US Customs got involved because I was violating health code laws and I was smuggling illegal wildlife into the country. Can I have my flute back?

Information on this playwright may be found at www.smithandkraus.com. Click on the AUTHORS tab.

THE NORTH POOL

Rajiv Joseph

Dramatic
Khadim: Late teens

Khadim, of Middle Eastern descent, but educated all over the world, has been detained in the Vice Principal's office for a detention. His only friend at the high school, a young girl, killed herself one month earlier. Here, he tells Dr. Danielson, the Vice Principal, about the last time he saw her.

KHADIM: She knew I could get her money. I know people who . . . Kids who . . .
   (beat)
These kids I know from Riyadh. Saudi Kids, Oil Kids. Way more money than me, and they throw these parties . . . And they like to bring in girls to be there, you know, to just wear a little dress and be sexy and get all fucked up with them. I told Lia about it, but not to . . . I didn't tell her about it so she would go there and do that! I told her because it was crazy. And Lia, she loved hearing about everything, all the stuff I've seen in my life, you know? She liked hearing about the world. But once she heard about these parties, she was intent. She would get intent on something, you know? She needed money. And they were going to pay her five thousand dollars to go to a *party*. She knew the deal. She knew what she was getting into.
   (becoming more upset)
I don't get invited to those parties. She went to it. It went all night long. I don't know what happened. She called me at like 5 in the morning. She was . . . She wanted me to come pick her up, and I went out to get her. She told me some corner that wasn't anywhere near the party. I don't know how she got there, I don't know what happened to her. And I kept having to call her back cause I couldn't find her. She'd say she was some place and then she

wouldn't be there. She'd say she was some other place, she wouldn't be there. And I was just driving around in circles. And then she was there. On some corner, in her little dress and no shoes and her feet were all dirty. She just got in and didn't say anything the whole way home. I couldn't even look at her. I wanted to tell her . . . I wanted to say to her . . .

(beat)

I pulled up to her Dad's house. Her Dad's shit-ass fucking piece of shit house and she got out.

(beat)

She said she got double the money because of her face. I was supposed to meet her at our spot, in the park, by the cliff. But I was late because I was buying that stupid flute. And she wasn't there, and I waited and waited and I started calling her. I called her and I called her and I . . . I still do. Her voice still answers.

(beat)

All I do anymore is sit around waiting for her! I sit around asking her *Where are you? Where are you? Where are you?* And if I had been on time, if I'd just gone straight there, if I hadn't sent her to the party, if I hadn't done anything, if I'd never met her, if I'd never seen her in my life . . .

Information on this playwright may be found
at www.smithandkraus.com. Click on the AUTHORS tab.

THE OTHER FELIX
Reina Hardy

Comic
The Other Felix: Late twenties to early thirties

Felix Bettleman is a professional gambler, and a recent victim of identity theft. But the thief is after more than Felix's name and credit rating—he's after Felix's soul. In this monologue, the Other Felix leaves a phone message for Felix's ex-girlfriend Lily in an attempt to further assimilate his identity by winning her love.

THE OTHER FELIX: Sir? Sir? Can I talk to you for a second? Sir? Sir? You can't play blackjack here anymore. You're kidding me. I just lost thousands of dollars—You can't play blackjack You must—surely you jest! I lost I just lost you must be kidding Sir, you can't—You can't You can't possibly mean that. I just lost thousands of dollars! Surely you're kidding! I'm serious. Oh well, um So it goes. I mean really it's the same old song just the same exchange between me who remains more or less constant with certain tweaks and innovations here and there and a slew of different characters of, you know, varying mettle so this this gentleman's mettle was not the toughest or scariest I had encountered On the other hand I felt guilty about being kind of obnoxious because I mean really he was civil and there was no need to be I just *had* lost thousands of dollars and was kind of sad and emotive which is, as they say in poker, showing weakness and no damn good. Anyway, I'm in Mississippi, where I am having the dickens of a time getting down. They don't like the action anywhere. And despite the fact that they win, every time I walk into a casino. I mean. Why do they bother to chase me out? I'm perplexed These and other quandaries, as well as the ongoing question of where is Lily Arkidner preoccupy me. I wake up dreaming about you and go to sleep the same way and I can't wait to see

you next week and yeah so I miss you is implicit in all
this and also a fact and goodnight goodnight.

Information on this playwright may be found
at www.smithandkraus.com. Click on the AUTHORS tab.

THE OTHER FELIX
Reina Hardy

Dramatic
Felix: Late twenties to early thirties

Felix Bettleman is a professional gambler, and a recent victim of identity theft. But the thief is after more than Felix's name and credit rating. He wants Felix's entire life—including his ex-girlfriend, Lily Arkidner. In this monolog, Felix chases after the Other Felix in an attempt to stop him from harming Lily.

FELIX: So I get into the car, and I go North. Like a compass. And always, just before me Just under the horizon There is a powder-blue mustang convertible that I never see what a jerk, to drive a convertible when you need to keep the hood up. It's like an insult to weather and to convertibles. I know because I've done it. It's coldth—the air smells sharp like New Year's Day. There are great silent trees and as the car makes low buzzing turns they sift snow down on my roof and it looks Like the sound of bells. They have auroras up here. I mean, not right now but there could be one at any moment and you sort of live with that knowledge like the knowledge that at any moment you could turn the corner and jam your fenders into a light blue mustang convertible with the hood up, and you'd both drift into a snow bank like lovers. Somehow it gets mixed up in my mind with the Aurora Borealis so that if one happens the other will happen, and if one doesn't happen neither will. Either I crash into a bank of powder blue light or I drive through the dark and the silent sound of bells for ever and ever. And as I drive I am always about to think of you and really, It's no different than the last time I was here when I thought of you at every moment And I wanted to see the northern lights and I never did. The sky above is deep and black, and then It's filled with snow. For no reason, I say a word

out loud. Angel. And then there is a hard white flutter
and something unfolds across my windshield and I do
crash without his help all-by-my-Felix and I think "Fuck.
I have conjured up some kind of justice and now here I
die" as the car glides in a slow circle and nestles itself
by the embankment like parallel parking itself in a bag
of marshmallows. I turn up, not-dead and the angel of
justice is just a large piece of white paper that had not
seemed previously important and that had unfolded its
wide white self as soon as my unconscious finger flicked
the windshield wipers At the first sight of snow. It's a
message. It's a town. It's an address. It's a hotel number.
It's not far. And then it happened. The sky just—explod-
ed. And I am looking right at an Aurora. It's that thing I
was waiting for. He must be looking at it too.

Information on this playwright may be found
at www.smithandkraus.com. Click on the AUTHORS tab.

The Patron Saint of Sea Monsters
Marlane Gomard Meyer

CALVIN, twenties to thirties
Dramatic

Calvin is on trial for killing his wife Marie. He is explaining it all to the judge.

CALVIN: Those bones in the sack, are her bones. Till I saw those bones I wasn't sure I would be able to turn myself in. Not being the kind of man who owns up to his mistakes. But when I saw those bones . . . I remembered, what a pretty girl she had been. How lively and sassy. And how much I loved her. *(Beat)* We were happy for a while, like kids are. But then I couldn't keep a job. Marie got fed up and decided to go to beauty school. When she went to apprentice in another town she started to have a life there, started to have new friends. She said all the men she worked with were gay but I didn't believe her. So one day I showed up at her job, drunk, got into a fight with this guy and broke his jaw. That tore it. She said she wanted a divorce. I said, fine! I let her pack up. She kissed me goodbye and she started to cry and I thought for a minute there she'd changed her mind but . . . she got in her car and drove away. I watched her, I waved. But . . . I knew she'd be back because I'd taken her license and registration! *(Smiles)* I had it all planned out, how I was gonna win her back. I bought a good, used, suit, got my hair professionally styled. And I borrowed money to buy her a nice ring. We'd just had a simple gold band when we got married . . . I wanted to get her a diamond. So, I went to the place where my half-brother, Jack, worked and he helped me pick out a beautiful ring. Big, shiny, and surprisingly inexpensive which should have tipped me off. I thought she'd come home pretty quick but it took three whole days. So that when she finally did come back, pissed as shit, instead of seeing me looking sharp, she saw me drunk, in an old dirty suit. But what I saw was worse. I saw that same dead eyed, disappointed look my Ma has when she sees me. But, being drunk, I thought I still had a chance. I pulled out the ring and showed her and she looked at it and she started laughing. Jack had sold me a zircon, if you don't know what that is, it's a fake Goddamned diamond. She could tell right away and she started in on how stupid I was and how she was glad to be rid of me. And it was there, in that great darkness between what I had dreamed of and how that dream was sailing down the shit hole that I became lost which I think is why I grabbed her by the neck and held on like I did. Or maybe it was because I did not want to be alone again. Do you understand? Because if there is one way to keep a woman with you forever it is to take the life she's going to live without you.

Information on this playwright may be found
at www.smithandkraus.com. Click on the AUTHORS tab.

THE PERFORMERS
David West Read

Comic
Chuck: Fifties

Chuck Wood, a legend in the porn film industry for many years, has just been named Best Male Performer at the Adult Film Awards, a surprise victory considering he was up against the likes of Blade Buttler, Little John Big Dong, Antonio Bonderass, Black Attack and Mandrew Rod-Dick. This is his acceptance speech.

CHUCK: Oh boy, I promised Black Attack I wouldn't cry, but . . . I was not expecting this.
(composing himself)
When I was a boy, I told my father that I was going to be the first Jew in the Basketball Hall of Fame, or a famous rock star, like Neil Diamond or Barry Manilow. My father looked at me and said, "Good for you, son, but some people don't give a shit about basketball. Some people don't even listen to music." I know I don't. *Pointless.* "But," he said, "there's one thing you can count on, one thing that unites every human being on this planet and it's this: Everybody fucks. So if you're best at fucking . . . you're the best human being."
(Beat)
I did not understand these words at the time—I was only six—but when I made my first adult film in 1978, I thought of my father. Not at the time of the shooting, of course, but in a general sense. The film was *Bad News Boner*. For my bone-tastic performance, I was awarded the Best New-Comer trophy; but sadly, my father died one week before the ceremony. I was devastated. I didn't know where to turn. I didn't understand that the answer was right in front of me.
(looking out)

It was you. My fellow performers. You've opened your hearts and your legs to me, and while I keep giving it to you, you keep giving *everything* to me. So Papa, if you can hear me up there. I want you to know this: I may be the best human being. I may be the best at fucking. But I'd be nothing without the people I've fucked. Thank you, have a wonderful night!

THE RECOMMENDATION
Jonathan Caren

Seriocomic
Dwight: Late twenties-early thirties,
African American

Dwight is in a small holding cell at a jail in Hollywood, talking to cellmate Adam Feldman, who has never been in such a hellhole and has no idea why he has been brought there by the cops. Dwight tells Adam why he has been arrested this time. Dwight has a hyper active fantasy life, and one of his fantasies is that he and Steven Spielberg are buddies.

DWIGHT: You know Spielberg? That's my boy. *E.T., Indiana Jones, Ghostbusters* shit. You like that movie? That's some funny ass shit, right? Se check it out. I'm chilling up in my Hollywood bungalow, kicking it, me and Steven, and this muthafuckin cop shows up. I know! I'm just minding my own business, *howling it up in my bowling alley*, and he says he's gotta talk to me. At first I'm like racking my brain at what's he's talking about, And then I remember the Korean woman. The mothafuckin Korean woman. This is over a *year* ago at the 76 on La Cienaga and Venice. I'm with this sweet-ass model from the Ukraine, you know, like one of them fashion runway models and shit, no joke. We about to go to dinner up and Mr. Chow's but my Bentley's running outta premium and Mr. Belvedere ain't driving me this week 'cause he's on vacation in the Caribbean, So I pull in, got my boy R. Kelly on the stereo and go to pay in cash, 'cause I'm doing alright, you know, gots me some money now. I hand the bitch a fifty. Say, "Fill me up on three." I go back, start fillin' my tank, but Bentley only fills like halfway. I go back to the Korean. I say, "Yo, somethin' wrong with your machine 'cause it only fillin' me up like twenty." And she says (Korean accent) "You give me twenny." I say, "Hell no, I gave you *fifty*. Check yo' register," so either bitch be scammin' me or she hid fifty so good now she cant's find it. I got my girl, I'm planning on spending that money on a primo bottle of Dom, but the chink won't give me my shit back. So instead of going ghetto, I have this Evian I be sippin' on. Just let it go in her direction. Wash her window clean so she can see shit better, know what I'm sayin'? But Korean calls the cops . . . So now I'm just waiting on Spielberg, 'cause he's gonna come on out here and sort all this shit out.

Information on this playwright may be found at www.smithandkraus.com. Click on the AUTHORS tab.

THE RECOMMENDATION

Jonathan Caren

Seriocomic
Dwight: Late twenties-early thirties,
African American

Dwight is in a small holding cell at a jail in Hollywood, talking to cellmate Adam Feldman, who has never been in such a hellhole and has no idea why he has been brought there by the cops. Adam is a personal assistant to a Hollywood producer and Dwight decides this is a golden opportunity to pitch a movie idea he has.

DWIGHT: I got a movie idea. This is some real blockbuster box office shit! You wanna hear my movie idea or not? OK, if you insist. It's called *Alien Trash Man*. See— homeboy gets kicked out of Earth. Fucking twenty-eight-dollar car stereo hold-up, know what I'm saying? The people on Earth send him up to this planet to get rid of him. But when he gets there, all them peoples are in like gold capes and wearing Versace eye patches. But since he's like, *normal* guy, they call him the alien and make him haul out trash. Every morning, he comes by five a.m. to collect their trash from their futuristic homes 'cause he's the *Alien Trash Man*. They be treatin' him like some lower species and shit. Then one day, he opens up the trashes to see what they all be throwin' out and he's like, "Holy shit, Batman!" Plasmas. Rolex! Fuckin' bling-a-ling diamonds all over the place. They say, "Go. Dump this out on bitch-ass Earth." 'Cause alien planet gots too much gold in it, know what I'm saying? He's like, "Uh, OK." So he takes their trash to his trash rocket. At first he's all worrying 'bout what they gonna do to him when he comes *back* landin' on Earth. But then *money* starts falling straight from the sky. People are all cheering. Dancing in the streets. Everybody collecting paychecks from nothing. No more unemployment Big

Mac breakfasts. Name him Prince of the Earth. Welcome back, Homecoming King. Strippers all stripping for free 'cause there ain't no need for money no more. *Alien. Trash. Man.*

Information on this playwright may be found at www.smithandkraus.com. Click on the AUTHORS tab.

THE SNOW GEESE
Sharr White

Dramatic
Arnie: Late teens

Arnie has been trying to make his mother understand that his recently deceased father has squandered the family fortune and that now they are left with nothing but debts. She has said she knows all about it. He responds, with the rest of the family present.

ARNIE: Do tell! Because this is the first *I've* heard of it! I mean—granted—something's apparently very wrong with me seeing as I do everything I can, everything you ask of me, and still it's like I'm this, this . . . *bruise* . . . around here, as if I'm some deaf and dumb idiot who can't figure out what language you're speaking! I just for once want us to say what we mean instead of speaking in all this, this . . . old-fashioned . . . *code* language—it is, it's complete *Victoriana*, mother. *I* don't know what you're aware of or what you're not! I mean we drove father's body all the way down to Syracuse with O'Neil between us and you made nothing but small talk the whole way. This was *after* I telephoned the funeral director down there who said he was terribly sorry but he'd want cash payment in advance to service our family, and he wouldn't make the trip up *here* without it, and anyway the family plot had been transferred to a Mr. Thom Rathbone two years ago. Well what the hell could all *that* mean? But there we are with dad trussed up and practically bouncing out of the back of the truck and allll she can talk about is the poor state of the road, and gosh she hoped the weather would co-operate for the service. And after that? We get to the bank. And Mr. Fillmore says he's sorry but he can't give us any cash for the preparations because—for one thing—father'd exhausted his line of credit in June. Line of credit? And for another thing, the bank had stopped honoring his checks in August, and there were several dozen creditors who were threatening action. I mean it was as if . . . I don't know what. As if I'd stepped outside to find the sky was green. Yet after *that,* mother made chirpy conversation on the way over to the house about the amount of black crepe in the attic and how she hoped there was enough to fit out a more fashionable mourning dress. Never a word about the fact that dad's body's in the truck and somehow he hasn't left enough money behind to buy so much as a coffin, let alone throw a proper service. And then! Thom Rathbone himself, new owner of the family burial plot, along with Julius Whoever—that fat friend of father's with the bulging left eye—come to the front door with bad checks in their hands—dad's not even stiff yet, those sons-of-bitches—and she— this was masterful— invites them in to have a drink, and so successfully does she small-talk them that they leave an hour later drunk and ashamed. And the kicker? Is that immediately after- wards she shouts up to O'Neil: wouldn't you know she's *just* remembered father's always spoken about a plain burial under the chestnut at the lodge. And do you know what we say to each other allllll the way back here? When just ten hours before I'd thought we were—all right, not wealthy—but at least solvent? Zero. Zee. Roe.

Information on this playwright may be found
at www.smithandkraus.com. Click on the AUTHORS tab.

THE SNOW GEESE

Sharr White

Dramatic
Arnie: Late teens

Arnie has gone over his deceased father's books and has learned that he has squandered the family fortune. He is explaining to the family what has happened to them, and how it has all been some sort of elaborate ruse to pamper his older brother Duncan, his parents' favorite.

ARNIE: The real story is that from the get-go he's betting his principle on stocks. The bank panic of '90. All zeroes. And then bang: here's the big one, ought-seven. Pretty much cleans him out. Which is when he brings in the accountant, who gobbles all the crumbs. For the last two years he was borrowing against *this* place to keep us in cash. But it's tapped out, spigot's turned off. And we haven't made a bank payment in . . . I don't know. Months. I always wondered why they didn't send me to join you at school. But now I realize they probably never had enough for both of us, even before the panic. What's funny is that I think in spite of father's reputation we were probably living pretty modestly; with mother, father, O'Neil and just a cook or so, usually. But about a week before you would come home on break, all these maids would appear. And they'd open the spare rooms, and the dust-covers would come off . . . I mean I suppose it might've been fun for them to pull out all the stops a few times a year. They didn't have to entertain. Just the spring and autumn shooting parties. Much easier to keep this . . . little world alive for you. And when you'd leave? So would most of the staff. I honestly never thought anything of it, that's just what happened. The world . . . opened up . . . when you came home. I remember one year, you arrive and everybody's all lined up, and you step out of the car like you always do, like royalty, you know, and you . . . have this . . . new smile. It's true, you look up and give everyone this grin, and all these . . . teeth. Just . . . pop out of your face. And sort of light up the afternoon—speaking of the world opening up. I mean you must've just learned that smile, because it wasn't there when we'd seen you at Thanksgiving, you must've developed it for some new friend—or it was a girl, I guess—but all I knew was, they sure weren't teaching that smile to me at Syracuse Academy. And we went to some Christmas gala that night, and I, I . . . just . . . trailed behind you, watching you try that new smile out. Teaching yourself how to cut a swath through the crowds with it, like some . . . glowing sword. And every head seemed to turn to you as you walked past. And people put their faces together and admired you. But then a few days later? You left back to school, and the staff went away, and the world closed up again. I remember thinking *well wait a minute, did everybody just . . . forget about me? When do I get to learn that?* I'd stand in front of the mirror at night and practice how to smile like that. Try to make my muscles do what yours do. Say to myself . . . *I* can make the world open up. *I* can make love come to me. *I* can make the future . . . fall at my feet. I really pretty much hate you. *(Beat)* Look, that's not true, Dunc, I actually for the most part . . . this sounds odd, but . . . I mean I'm kind of in awe of you. Of what you are. And *that's* what I hate.

Information on this playwright may be found
at www.smithandkraus.com. Click on the AUTHORS tab.

The Totalitarians

Peter Sinn Nachtrieb

Dramatic
Jeffrey: Mid thirties to early forties

Jeffrey lives in Nebraska, where he is a doctor. Here, he is telling his wife about an angry young patient.

JEFFREY: This guy came into my office the other day with a lump near his ribs. Convinced it was Cancer. Everyone thinks their lump is Cancer. And I try to reassure them. Most "cancers" are fatty cysts. I'll run tests, insurance-willing, but assume the best. Assume your body has only produced a harmless sac until proven otherwise. Most people feel better when I say that but this boy . . . yelled at me. Loudly. Said my attitude is "what is wrong with Nebraska." That if we really want to cure what ails our state, we need to assume the worst. When the "future hangs in the balance we must fight with everything we got!" And then he half shouted half growled. Like a Scottish warrior. Fist in the air. The nurse came in. It was very intense. His body is infested. Mass like a Cauliflower. Cancer spread to his bones, blood, everywhere and nothing can stop it. Surgery, chemo, radiation, nada. A bright man with a "mission." So much he wants to do with his life but Mr. Cancer doesn't care. Mr. Cancer has no morals. It just wants to grow. So what if you're a dreamer . . . There's a Mr. Something coming for all of us. I have to tell him tomorrow. I really don't want to tell him. What do I even say?

THE TOTALITARIANS
Peter Sinn Nachtrieb

Dramatic
Ben: Mid-twenties

Ben, a revolutionary, tells his doctor, Jeffrey, about a secret organization that is planning to take over Nebraska. He wants Jeffrey to join him in the resistance.

BEN: I used to have an older brother! Billy. Billy The Bestest. Billy The Beefcake. Everyone wants to be Boyfriends with Billy. Quarterback, Eagle Scout, Mathelete. Total opposite of me. And everyone loved him, told him how amazing he was, gave him twenty percent off. And my mom licked his feet like they were made of salami while I never even got to eat my favorite cereal other than that one time. And Billy loved his privilege. Started to believe he'd earned it, that he deserved things more than others. "Equality is what lazy people want, taintface. You could be just like me if you worked as hard as I do." And when I tried to inform him about the illusion of fairness he punched me in the face. And that was only the beginning. Billy became a bully. Weakness and difference disgusted him so much he would beat the crap out of anybody who was, a.k.a. me. He *believed* he was enforcing the rightful order of things. And *they* just let it happen. Teachers, authorities, my shit parents. Impressed by his strength, his viciousness, the fear he could instill in the disenfranchised. He was offered a full scholarship to Yale. I had one friend growing up. Edgerton Lansing. A scrawny quiet translucent boy with a cleft palette and a smell. Billy beat him up so hard he almost died. And while Edgey was still in the ICU, Billy went around town boasting about what he had done to this kid. And that he did it because the kid was a "fag." Quite a few "fags" lived in our town. "Fags" who all held a quiet, simmering rage in their souls that had been intensifying for years, waiting for one injustice too many to blow the lid off the pot. Rage felt by Billy's little brother, a.k.a. me, who knew the exact dark alley his older brother took home at night from the Kwik Stop and knew precisely what online chat room to share that information. When they found Billy, his body was barely even a body. Pounded so flat you could do yoga on him. And I'm the reason it happened. That's when I knew I was an activist. That is what a community coming together can do. There is a very powerful and potent amount of rage out there, waiting to be tapped. All it takes is a little spark . . . boom. And even the most powerful forces on the planet will come crumbling down. That's what we're going to do.

THE TRIBUTE ARTIST
Charles Busch

Seriocomic
Jimmy: Fifties

Jimmy, a professional female impersonator (he refers to himself as a "tribute artist"), is trying to con Christina out of her inheritance, a posh townhouse, by posing as her aunt, who has actually died. Here, he spins a fantastic tale of his past, none of which is true.

JIMMY: Vienna. The winters were so lovely. The powdery snow covering the Wienerwald. We had to escape. We had to flee on a midnight train, passports purloined on the black market. Think *Three Comrades. The Mortal Storm.* Margaret Sullavan. My father moved the lamps, everything to Sweden. Stockholm. I don't even remember Vienna. I was so young and traumatized. Anyway, it was a magical kind of store, all amber light and crystal beading on the lampshades, right out of *The Shop Around the Corner.* A 1940 Lubitsch comedy. Margaret Sullavan was in that one too. Well, you don't make a killing selling finials on the fjord. But that didn't stop my father from having a wild old time, particularly after my mother died. He was more like a younger brother than a father. I wouldn't call my father a listener. But when he was around, he was a lot of fun. And he could be very affectionate. I used to sleepwalk when I was little and they'd always find me curled up in the laundry basket in the linen closet holding his shirt collar close to my nose. There was something about the cool crispness of the collar and the clean smell of the starch that I loved. Maybe it was just him. At a certain point I had to cut him out of my life. You just couldn't depend on him. I once developed a terrible stye on my eye. The kind that won't go away by itself. It had to be operated on but he couldn't get around to making the appointment for the surgery. It kept getting bigger

and bigger and became sort of carnival side show freak-
ish. Finally a teacher of mine contacted someone from
the Child Welfare Department, who had to step in and
set up the appointment to remove the chalazion, that's
what they call it, and then make sure my father took me
there. So at twelve years old, I decided to live with my
grandmother . . . in Lisbon. I wanted to. I had to. He
was fun but dangerous. Later on, when I was grown up
. . . and working in Paris, my father tried very hard to
make amends. He seemed grateful for any bone I threw
at him. He was very proud of what I'd done with my
life. Surprising, considering my profession. You know,
fashion. I wanted to be affectionate with him and sort of
faked it. You see I can just turn off all feeling like a light
switch. Maybe that's my one minute video self-portrait.
Me turning off the light switch on a beautiful but highly
impractical antique lamp.

THE TRIBUTE ARTIST
Charles Busch

Seriocomic
Rodney: Forties to fifties

Rodney is a shady character who has been trying to bilk Jimmy, Rita and Christine out of the townhouse owned by a recently deceased woman whom Jimmy, a professional female impersonator (he calls himself a "tribute artist") has been impersonating. Jimmy has the hots for Rodney. He has managed to lure everyone upstairs for an orgy of sorts, in hopes of having sex with Rodney, who is as definitely straight as Rita is definitely gay. Christina has been living off the stolen credit cards of a dead friend. A lot of what Rodney says about himself here is fiction. Anyway, he's storing a dead body in the fur vault, has been found out and has had enough of these crazy people, who have threatened to report him to the police.

RODNEY: I'll be gone before any of you get up. Where I'll go, what will happen to me, I don't know. Not that any one of you give a damn about my situation, but here I am raised by a bi-polar heroin addict, emotionally and sexually abused since I can remember, caught in the web of a predatory older woman and being so crushed by her merciless narcissism that I wound up a drug addict on skid row, only to be years later, jerked out of a hard won sobriety by an emotionally disturbed gender bending teenager, with the promise of a kind of spiritual salvation but find myself instead sexually harassed and pursued by a grifter drag queen and a mid-western credit card scam artist, who I did my best to encourage and build sexual confidence in herself, and in return, haven't received an ounce of sympathy or understanding that perhaps I had valid personal reasons for "creating accidents" that might *possibly* have harmed her but didn't, and anyway should be proof positive that rather than being a victim of misfortune, she actually lives under a lucky star to have escaped injury so often, but of course, no thanks come my way and indeed to top it off, I'm stripped naked and forced against my will to endure an excruciatingly painful blow job from a man hating lesbian. Well, as they say, life isn't fair. I'm going. I can't go soon enough. I have witnessed unspeakable horrors in all four corners of the world; slavery, torture, cannibalism, but I have never encountered a more vile, hypocritical, insincere, morally corrupt group than those living under this hateful roof and if there's any justice, I hope it caves in on all of you. I'll have someone pick up the body tomorrow. Good night.

THE UNAVOIDABLE DISAPPEARANCE OF TOM DURNIN
Steven Levenson

Dramatic
James: Twenty-six

James tells Katie, a woman he has just started dating, about Addison, his girlfriend, who left him. We find out later that James, like his father, is a chronic liar. In fact, Addison was his wife

JAMES: No, it's fine. It's just . . .Huh. Well. To make a long story short, I guess, she met—Addison, her name was Addison, *is* Addison, she didn't die or anything—she met someone else, a guy at work, she worked at J. Crew, and so did he. They had the same shift, apparently. And she fell in love with him, I guess, is essentially, that's the basic story. She fell in love, and she told me about it. And she told me they were moving to Portland, Oregon, which she'd never even been to. I'd been there, and I told her it wasn't that great. It rains a lot. Not as much as Seattle or something like that, but enough. And she has issues with, when it's winter and the days are shorter, she gets depressed. So I told her that Portland would just be the worst for that. It would really be a bad decision, purely just, objectively speaking, mental health-wise. So I told her that. And that I loved her. I was in love with her, still. I thought we had a real sort of, a future. And she told me, thank you, that was nice. She loved me, too. In a way, in a certain way. But not the way she loved Van—that was the guy's name, Van. So she was sorry, and she appreciated what I said about the rain and the winter, but it didn't matter to her. As long as she was in love. As long as she was happy. And then she, uh . . . then she left.

Information on this playwright may be found at www.smithandkraus.com. Click on the AUTHORS tab.

The Unavoidable Disappearance of Tom Durnin
Steven Levenson

Dramatic
James: Twenty-six

James' father, Tom, has just been released from prison, where he did time for financial fraud. Tom has been trying to reconstitute his family, and his life. James will have none of it, and lays into his father for the pain he has caused his family.

JAMES: You really, you actually believe that you're the victim here, don't you? You actually believe that. I had the FBI come to my dorm room. They took my car. They took my credit cards. They took the TV, they took the computer. And you weren't there. I had to get on a bus, book Mom into the Holiday Inn, she had three suitcases with everything she owned in them. She was going on and on about the unfairness, the political, it was all political, there was no evidence, it was a travesty, it was injustice. On and on and on. The whole night. She was shaking. Her whole body was shaking. And where were you, Dad? And Annie. Annie's six-months pregnant. Her three-year old son is crying, he wants to know why his grandfather is on all the TV channels. She's having panic attacks every three hours, they need her to calm down, they think she's going to deliver the baby prematurely, she can't calm down, they want to give her drugs, she doesn't want drugs, she won't take drugs, she can't calm down. She doesn't know if her husband is going to have a job in the morning, because suddenly everybody who has anything to do with you, everybody who has ever so much as *met* you, suddenly everybody has become a suspect, because you are *toxic*.

Information on this playwright may be found
at www.smithandkraus.com. Click on the AUTHORS tab.

T.I.C. (Trenchcoat In Common)
Peter Sinn Nachtrieb

Comic
Terrence: Thirties to forties

Terrence, a flasher, is talking into a video camera he's just discovered in his apartment building, placed by a teenaged girl named Kid who is writing a blog about her neighbors. He is charming, but a little creepy.

TERRENCE: Do not be scared of me. I am but a humble exhibitionist. I come from a family of exhibitionists, the craft and traditions passed down from generation to generation. My mother and father taught me to love my body and how to harness the power that it has on other people as they walk on the street in their myopic fogs. A little skin and a "boo" and I used to feel like I'd made a little impact upon the world. These modern days have been harder for flashers like me, for those of us who cling to the traditional means. The competition is enormous. Last week I executed my boldest maneuver, the Ghipetto, flawlessly to a group of Ohioan tourists. But their only response was a polite cough and a single digital group photo. It's getting to harder to heighten the senses of my brothers and sisters out there. The threshold of taboo gets higher and higher. Perhaps I am becoming obsolete. Oh look at me with my jabber jabber. I think we might be playing for the same team. I look forward to our encounter.

TRAVEN

Don Nigro

Dramatic
Traven: Fifties

Traven, a man in his fifties, is in his house deep in the Mexican jungle, sometime in the mid-twentieth century, speaking to Marisela, a girl in her twenties, who has been searching for him. She believes he is the famous, mysterious writer B. Traven, author of The Treasure of the Sierra Madre, whose identity has long been disputed. He claims to be somebody else. She wants to translate Traven's collected works and bring out a uniform final edition. He denies being the elusive author, and has begun working to gradually to undermine and eventually destroy her sense of what's real.

TRAVEN: How do you know anything? How do you know what's a final text? The only way you can have a final text is to murder the author. But in order to kill a man, you've got to find him. And how do you find him when you're not even sure who he is, or even if he exists? And if he does exist, if he is not a figment of your imagination, I suspect this B. Traven person would prefer to apply the sort of philosophical anarchism displayed in his work to the work's textual history as well. You want to make clear and uniform the collected works of a person who's spent his whole life deliberately creating obfuscations. It's like clear cutting the jungle. He likes the jungle. He's created a collected works which is a jungle. People like you come in and try to establish order. But the way you establish order is to kill the very beast you profess to worship. Everybody wants to kill somebody. Are you people really too stupid to understand that at the core of these works is a massive celebration of anarchy? That any attempt to create uniformity is to compromise the very nature of the author's vision itself? That's why you've come here, you know. You thought you came here to find B. Traven.

To save B. Traven. Maybe even to fuck B. Traven. But now that you're here, it's clear that what you really want is to kill him. To make uniform is to destroy. You came to cut out the jungle he's created. But the jungle is a lot bigger than you are. The jungle will devour you. The jungle always wins, in the end.

TRAVEN

Don Nigro

Dramatic
Traven: Fifties

Traven, a man in his fifties, is in his house deep in the Mexican jungle, sometime in the mid-twentieth century, speaking to Marisela, a girl in her twenties, who has been searching for him. She believes he is the famous, mysterious writer B. Traven, author of The Treasure of the Sierra Madre, whose identity has long been disputed. He claims to be somebody else. She wants to translate Traven's collected works and bring out a uniform final edition. He denies being the elusive author, and has begun working to gradually undermine and eventually destroy her sense of what's real. She's just told him she doesn't want to play any games. He defends himself by questioning her motives and undermining her confidence and sense of self.

TRAVEN: Then you want to be dead. Because there are only two choices: games or death. There is no place in between. All straight lines are an illusion. Everything in the universe is twisted, like a labyrinth. But there's no monster at the center. There's nothing there. And they can't take anything from you if there's nothing there to begin with. You wake up from a dream, and everything you thought was real is gone, and that is the only reality. Cover up the mirrors. I think we're done here. What do you really want with me? You're a beautiful young woman. You could do just about anything. You could have just about anybody. Why do you care who I am? Why are you bothering with Traven at all? Because you love his work? That's rubbish. Nobody in her right mind would come all the way out here in the middle of the jungle because she liked somebody's work. You're drawn to this B. Traven person precisely because you can't put him in a box and dismiss him. He's not one of these and he's not one of those. You don't know what he is. It's the very fact that he's nobody, that he's a liar, that allows you to project onto him whatever you want to see. You're a girl looking for a man with no face. Because you're afraid to love a real person. You'd rather love someone who's imaginary. Preferably somebody who'll hurt you. Because a man who will go out of his way to hurt you is at least dealing with you. A man who professes to love you isn't even seeing you. He's in love with somebody in his head. A man who hurts you will have to pay attention to you. Otherwise, how will he know how to hurt you the most?

TROPICAL HEAT
Rich Orloff

Comic
Eric: Twenties to thirties

Tropical Heat, *set on a South Seas island during the 1920's,
is an over-the-top comedy about a grandiose missionary
who falls for woman of easy virtue, and the others who
frequent the island's only hotel and bar. Eric is an aspiring
tormented artist who lacks both torment and the courage to
paint. When he finally finishes his first painting, he admits
to Pops, the hotel's owner, that neither the painting nor his
life has turned out as planned.*

ERIC: Oh, who am I kidding? It's a terrible painting. The
colors create neither the illusion of flesh nor an imagi-
native commentary on the essence of the body. Not
only does the painting lack dimensionality, it doesn't
compensate by providing the sort of creative perspective
which bypasses literalism to provide hitherto unseen or
unnoticed truths. The painting isn't even bland, it's life-
less, as if the painter felt neither the power of paint nor
the awe of nature. Oh God, oh God, for years I yearned
to create, and now my biggest fear has come true: I have
no talent! My mind questions if life is worth living. I'm
finally consumed with pure, unendurable torment! But
wait! *Wait!* Even though this is the darkest moment of
my existence, as I let go of my lifelong dream, a thought
begins shyly to take form . . . Yes. Yes . . . An incredible
thought. Suddenly I feel a brilliant clarity about how I
should spend my life. I will become . . . I will become
. . . I am becoming . . . *a critic.* Suddenly my life has
purpose! To become a critic! If I can't feel torment, at
least I can bring torment to others! Oh, to wake up each
morning ready to use my God-given gift of pointing out
flaws that people might not otherwise notice. To mock
and humiliate in a way that makes rejection entertain-

ing. To dole out approval with such scarcity that anyone creative will yearn for a kind word from me. What other life could compare to that? Thank you, Pops. If you hadn't pushed me to paint this monstrosity, I would've never reached this moment. Whoever I become I owe to you. And by the way, you need to spruce this place up. It lacks conceptual unity, and it's drab. God, I love the sound of my own voice! Here I come, world; those with fragile egos should hide!

UNDISCOVERED PLACES
D. Richard Tucker

Dramatic
Dan: Forty-nine

After finding out he has a daughter, now an adult, Dan contacts her and arranges a meeting that does not go well. Because of his awkwardness and inability to connect, the evening ends in rejection. Here, Dan relates the experience—his feelings as he got to meet his own flesh and blood, and his disappointment in the outcome.

DAN: I've just been leaving humiliating voice mails for a girl in Denver and in hopes that I may drive her farther away than I already have. I just . . . . I don't know. When I saw her there . . . it was different. She seemed new and . . . familiar all at the same time. Her nose is just like my mom's. The way she talked, was kind of like Candice—when she was younger. And she just had something . . . I don't know—she just drew me to herself. So there I was, trying not to say anything stupid, and trying to sound smart and fatherly, and somewhere in the midst of that, she sucked me in and I fell in love with her. Like . . . . I started worrying about her, thinking about every aspect of her life, and looking for ways to ensure that nothing ever happened to her, you know nothing bad, or anything that would cause her disappointment. I wanted to audit her home owner's insurance policy, and measure the thickness of her brake pads. I wanted to be there to check out the guys who might drop by. I wanted to give her advice on her 401K. All of this just welled up inside me, over a person I had just met, and I didn't know how to deal with my feelings, so I bit my tongue, and watched as she walked out of my life.

Information on this playwright may be found
at www.smithandkraus.com. Click on the AUTHORS tab.

WARRIOR CLASS
Kenneth Lin

Dramatic
Nathan: Fifties

Nathan is a behind the scenes mover and shaker in New York State politics. He is backing an idealistic young Republican Assemblyman named Julius Lee who is running for Congress. Problem is, Julius has a skeleton in his closet, his college girlfriend, Holly, whom he sexually harassed when she dumped him, genuinely menacing her. Holly wants a job for her husband in return for her silence. Nathan is trying to broker a deal with her

NATHAN: I'd like to hope that I could see that people change. *(Beat)* People can become who they were meant to be.
    (He laughs.)
You know we didn't even really send anyone to campaign for him? Didn't think he had a shot. DiLorenzo, the Democrat that had Julius's seat, was there for like twenty years, hugely popular. Any Republican who ever tried to touch that seat got slaughtered and never came back. Julius wasn't even running at first. The pastor in his church asked him to do it. That's how he got in. No political action committees, not a single PAC behind him. We gave Julius fifteen thousand dollars worth of canned tele-marketing from Rick Lazio and Al D'Amato. Come on.
    (Eye-roll.)
And six weeks before election day, he gives that speech. Music. "Has it been that long since I've heard it?" "Have I ever really heard it?" And I met him, and he's for real. That just doesn't happen. Me and my guys are trying to get him on some big money committee and he's fighting me 'cause he wants join some empty cupboard committee to overturn bad laws that no one

cares about. He's breaking all the rules, and believe me, that's a very good thing. Look, I'm ... I'm sorry he ... hurt you, Holly. It sounds very awful. But, it was a long time ago. Work with us. We can make a lot of things right again. This happens all the time. I have two talks like this a month. Half the people in office are there because they're nursing someone's skeleton. And a lot of them get there and they do good work. It's actually what they were meant to do. We can do something here. I just don't see the sense, Holly. Ruining things for him, how does it help you? Your position's not a strong as you'd like to think it is. Your husband's a crook and you're a desperate housewife with a history of anxiety disorders. Are you listening to me? I think you should take this deal.

WARRIOR CLASS
Kenneth Lin

Dramatic
Nathan: Forties

Nathan is a mover and shaker in New York state politics. The Republican Party establishment was backing an idealistic Assemblyman named Julius Lee, who was going to run for Congress until his college girlfriend came out of the woodwork with charges that he went insane when she dumped him and menaced her. Reluctantly, the party has dumped Julius. Here, Nathan waxed philosophical to him.

NATHAN: Hey, you know, it's not the end of the world. Racing and wagering is going to keep you plenty busy. You'll be getting your Assembly campaign going in about a year. Make another great speech; fill up the war chest. Bring in a few more big guns. Make the right votes. Okay? *(Pause)* Okay. You popped your cherry. Welcome to Politics For Real. Four years, who knows what's going to happen. Everything could be different. It's guaranteed things will be different. By then you and Annie'll have a baby, maybe two. It'll be beautiful. Look, I know you two are having a rough patch right now, but trust me, she's not going to leave you. I talked to her sister. She's just upset right now. So are you. You're going to see. This is all normal. You'll find a way to make it work. You should have Annie talk to Diane. You know, I counted it once, I think that I stay in my actual house for two months total out of every year. You want to know why? Diane doesn't like it when I'm home. Oh, we love each other and she's happy when she sees me. But, I can tell, after a few days at home it's like the British have re-instated the Quartering Act. The kids were the same way too. Used to be they'd run to see me; then they'd run to their rooms; now they're out there in the world in some foxhole or something hoping I forgot them. Diane used to tell me that I wasn't fit for the house. That they were civilians and that I was from a warrior class. How do you like that? In the end, everyone finds their own way and it all works out great. It's fine. I can see this is killing you, Julie. I get it. Believe me I get it. For guys like us, you're either winning or you're dying, and you came here, right? You sailed across the wine-dark sea to seek Elysian Fields and now it's like you're just polishing the armor. But, you got to trust me. There's a lot of ways to win.

WHY WE LEFT BROOKLYN OR THE DINNER PARTY PLAY
Matt Freeman

Seriocomic
Charlie: Thirty-four

Charlie is attending a farewell dinner party for his best friend. During the party, he attempts to explain why he doesn't try yoga to a particularly insistent friend.

CHARLIE: I can't move my knees more than 90 degrees. I had bone spurs all over my body when I was a kid. My knees looked like someone had smashed them with a hammer. Got them all shaved off, in a really painful procedure, between my freshman and sophomore years in college. Shaved bone right off my knees, my shoulders, my back. There are some little scars, but it's hard to tell. Even so, I still can't do a lot of things. Like sit Indian style. Honestly, it was this crazy situation because, like, imagine that you're already thirteen and you have zits and you're skinny and you're in Minnetonka, Minnesota. Everything is a fucking pool party or a party on a boat. Everyone wants you to go out with your shorts or with your shirt off and cook brats or whatever. That's the thing, like most of the year it's freezing and the weather in dangerous, and the rest of the time, around the lake, it's like we're living on the beach. So I would go through all these weird, I mean weird, twisted lies to avoid showing up anywhere in a bathing suit. Machinations. Elaborate scams. Invent funerals, killing off lots of imaginary cousins and uncles. I literally got in a car and drove home once, just disappeared from a party, because I was at this girl's house and they gave me her brother's bathing suit when I told them I forgot mine at home. I was in the bathroom, holding these shorts, trapped like an animal. I thought, 'Fuck it, there's no way out.' Drove away, just to keep people from seeing my actual body. So, I don't know, lots of kinds of exercise, that rely on flexibility, are challenging for me. Painful.

Why We Left Brooklyn or the Dinner Party Play
Matt Freeman

Seriocomic
Harry: Thirty-seven

Harry is attending a dinner party with his girlfriend Leanna. He's a well-known chef in New York, having appeared on television. He spins a wild story to describe the new restaurant he's just opened.

HARRY: Our cuisine is fear-based. *(Pause)* Basically, if you know anything about venison, I'm not assuming you don't, but if you know anything about it, you'll know that when a deer realizes it's about to be killed, when it senses mortal danger, its adrenal gland goes into overdrive so that it can more quickly escape. It voids its bowels, the way you would if you were afraid, its mouth goes dry, all sorts of changes occur. To me, that slightly, almost imperceptible sense of extra blood sugar and chemistry adds something essential. Terrified animals, in essence, sort of season themselves. It's a light, frothy hint of horror. It's like those moments in a slasher film just before the monster jumps out. That delicious feeling, only more, actually, delicious. *(Pause)* So anyway, what New York Magazine liked about us is that we're inspired by the idea that food isn't meant to be treated like it's wearing a white dress. We humiliate pork with paprika, humble ham with local honey, tease trout with turmeric. We serve whole calf head with a crown of rosemary thorns. I actually serve bowls of eyeballs, in a tear-infused reduction. *(Pause)* That's a popular one, actually. You're aghast. But look, you know how much backlash Jonathan Safron Foer got with his smug book about being a vegetarian and also a wealthy prima-donna novelist? It's like the world is begging to kick him in the nuts, but they don't want to eat McDonalds to do it. So here's my shop, and I'm not fucking around, it's good food. And we're not being weak-kneed about making sure your cow is smiling right before we shave its head off and feed it to you. We're saying that every restaurant is Faces of Death so let's all give that fact a big hug and a kiss.

WHY WE LEFT BROOKLYN OR THE DINNER PARTY PLAY
Matt Freeman

Seriocomic
Jason: Early thirties

Jason is hosting a farewell dinner party with friends in Brooklyn. In order to explain his dislike for the word "fresh" he recounts a trip he took with an old girlfriend.

JASON: When I was dating Karen and we drove out to Pennsylvania to visit my Mom. Karen was from, you know, northern New Jersey and had weird ideas about why some people got rich and others didn't. She was one of those people who believed that wealth and brains and hard work were in direct correlation, even though her Dad ran a sweat shop and my Mom taught other people's kids. I guess managing a sweat shop is like, harder work. We stopped at this one diner and the food was fucking Pennsylvania diner food. Normal, unimpressive, stock food. We were thinking about dessert, and then Karen asks the waitress about the pie. She's like "I'm thinking about getting a slice of that pie." The waitress looks at her like, "Uh huh." So Karen's like "Is it . . . good?" The waitress is this fucking who-knows-how-many-times-over young mother who is just waiting for Karen to pick "pie or no pie." Karen's like "Is it *fresh?*" The waitress clearly continues to not care. Finally Karen, looking totally out of her depth, says "*Sell* me this pie." As if the waitress is not doing her job properly, as if their status is not properly being accounted for in this situation. It's how she said it. It's how people *say* it. "Are those fresh tomatoes?" "Are those cherries fresh?" "Oh these peaches are so fresh." It's an indicator of a subtle god-damned palette. Demanding freshness is just a code for a belief that you deserve the best, accept only the best. It's a nose-in-the-air word. You might as well walk into someone else's house and say "What's that smell?"

WILD

Crystal Skillman

Dramatic
Jordy: Nineteen

Jordy, a neurotic guy from Kansas interning to be a stock broker who is desperate in his search for any kind of love in his life, finds himself alone on a beach late at night with Bobby who he's been flirting with in the office.

JORDY: You have no idea what—I don't know what to do after Mesirow—I go home—when I go home and—I don't know what to tell them, you know? I'm pretty sure they're going to fire me. I've been pretty much wandering around the north conference room where they ring in Patty, all the people they fire on their fucking list—the meeting room where I put out coffee and I hear them deciding who is on their firing list—the names—knowing that they're going to fire me. And then there's another internship next year and finishing college and I'm supposed to know this is what I want to do Bobby! And I have no idea what I'm looking for! Not a clue! Wherever I walk into—Pippin's sweating my balls off—anywhere—I walk in and it's packed and I can barely move with people but I'm looking for someone like me. Someone like me right but everyone I look at they *know* what the fuck they want to do, where they want to go. And where do I go? Go to a club—Angels and Kings or Downtown Bar and even then, even with everyone trying to go home with someone there's some kind of drive—some kind of passion. I don't know what to do with mine. And I go home with someone. I always go home with someone. Girls, guys, I don't give a fuck. I'm fucking someone and I don't even know I'm there.

Information on this playwright may be found at www.smithandkraus.com. Click on the AUTHORS tab.

WILD

Crystal Skillman

Dramatic
Peter: Twenty-five

Peter, stock broker whose father is dying and whose own infidelity has set a chain of events into motion, including his own lover Bobby now cheating on him, is encouraged by Vin, a calm "zen-like" young college student, relaxing on the beach to share what's upsetting him.

PETER: My father. He's sick. He's really fucking sick. Sure you can say it's prostate cancer but it's not even just one thing—drinking like—and his body is literally falling apart. Has been. Piece by piece. Not that he gives a shit. When I brought Bobby home? I didn't prepare them. We just walked in. As if we could walk in and everything would be ok. Bobby has no idea—he's just like, "They're shit, forget them!" Bobby's family they're—they love him. Bobby's mom and dad, his brother Ted rally around him like—and mine? My sister Ellen tells me I'm going to hell. She doesn't say those words but she leaves reports of misery on my phone. Sends photos of dear old dying dad. Today's message? "This is it." So I fucking have patience. I get it together. I take my lunch break. I go to the hospital. I can't get past the doors. I look at them and other people going in and out and I know I'm on some list—like "don't let him in" but I know if I *wanted* to – if I *want*—they couldn't stop me—but it's me—I can't go in there—me—so —so—here's the thing—if you asked my family to cut me up and said to my fucked up dying father what part of your son do you like? What one fucking thing of your son—what redeeming quality do you love? He wouldn't pick any part of me. They wouldn't pick any part of me. I hurt them because of who I am. I hurt Bobby - I fucked someone else. A woman. I don't know why. I fucked it up. And I'm telling you this because I hurt people and I don't know why. I can't change what I did and I can't fix it. I'm just trying and it's not good enough. Not any piece of me is good enough and I don't know what to do.

Information on this playwright may be found at www.smithandkraus.com. Click on the AUTHORS tab.